Reef, Royal &

India

Florence
& Blade

Sheba
(See page 18 for
alternative version)

George

Piper &
Musk

Piper
(Child's version
on page 10)

Zebra & Blade

13

Florence

14

Royal

16

Hawk
& India

Reef &
Sheba

Hawk

19

Lola
(Alternative version
shown on page 6)

20

Bella

Gem

Rupert

Rupert

Rowan Chenille Collection

Knitting instructions
Index

Design	Patt No	Page
Bella	17	48
Bilberry Cushion	18	48
Blade	5	31
Blossom	10	38
Florence	6	32
Gem	15	47
George sweater	14	44
Glow Cushion and Blanket	20	49
Hawk	3	28
India	11	39
Jet sweater and cardigan	13	42
Lola	7	34
Lush Cushion	19	48
Musk	12	41
Piper	4	29
Reef	2	26
Royal	8	36
Rupert	16	47
Sheba	9	37
Zebra	1	24
Zebra Cushion	21	49
Information Page		50

Design number 1

Zebra

KIM HARGREAVES

YARN
Rowan Chunky Chenille

	S	M	L	
Two colour version				
A Parchment 383	6	6	6	x100gm
B Black 367	5	5	5	x100gm
One colour version	11	11	11	x100gm

(Photographed in 382 Lush)

NEEDLES
1 pair 4mm (no 8) (US 6) needles
1 pair 4¹/₂mm (no 7) (US 7) needles

BUTTONS - 6

TENSION
16 sts and 24 rows to 10 cm measured over st st using 4¹/₂mm (US 7) needles.

Two colour version
BACK
Cast on 85 (89: 95) sts using 4mm (US 6) needles and yarn A.

Work in garter st for 2.5 cm, ending with a WS row.
Change to 4¹/₂mm (US 7) needles.
Beg and ending rows as indicated and using the **intarsia** technique described on the information page, work 16 (20: 24) rows in patt from body chart which is worked entirely in st st, beg with a K row and ending with a WS row.
Keeping chart correct, shape side seams by dec 1 st at each end of next and every foll 6th row until 69 (73: 79) sts rem.
Cont without further shaping until chart row 76 (80: 86) has been worked, thus ending with a WS row.
Inc 1 st at each end of next and every foll 4th row until there are 85 (89: 95) sts.
Cont without further shaping until chart row 114 (122: 130) has been worked, thus ending with a WS row.
Shape armholes
Keeping chart correct, cast off 4 sts at beg of next 2 rows. 77 (81: 87) sts.
Dec 1 st at each end of next 5 rows, then on every foll alt row until 61 (65: 71) sts rem.
Cont without further shaping until chart row 170 (178: 186) has been worked, thus ending with a WS row.
Shape back neck and shoulders
Cast off 6 (6: 7) sts at beg of next 2 rows. 49 (53: 57) sts.
Next row (RS): Cast off 6 (7: 8) sts, patt until there are 10 (11: 12) sts on right needle and turn, leaving rem sts on a holder.
Work each side of neck separately.
Cast off 4 sts at beg of next row.
Cast off rem 6 (7: 8) sts.
With RS facing, rejoin yarn to rem sts, cast off centre 17 sts, patt to end.
Work to match first side, reversing shapings.

POCKET LININGS (make 2)
Cast on 20 sts using 4¹/₂mm (US 7) needles and yarn A.
Beg with a K row, work 36 (38: 40) rows in st st.
Break yarn and leave sts on a holder.

LEFT FRONT
Cast on 43 (45: 48) sts using 4mm (US 6) needles and yarn A.
Work in garter st for 2.5 cm, ending with a WS row.
Change to 4¹/₂mm (US 7) needles.
Beg and ending rows as indicated, work 16 (20: 24) rows in patt from body chart, thus ending with a WS row.
Keeping chart correct, shape side seam by dec 1 st at beg of next and every foll 6th row until 39 (42: 45) sts rem.
Work 1 (5: 3) rows, thus ending with a WS row.
Place pocket
Next row (RS): [Patt 2 tog] 0 (1: 0) times, patt 7 (7: 11) sts, slip next 20 sts on a holder, patt across 20 sts of first pocket lining, patt 12 (13: 14) sts. 39 (41: 45) sts.
Cont foll chart, dec 1 st at beg of every foll 6th row from previous dec until 35 (37: 40) sts rem.
Cont without further shaping until chart row 76 (80: 86) has been worked, thus ending with a WS row.
Inc 1 st at beg of next and every foll 4th row until there are 43 (45: 48) sts.

Cont without further shaping until chart row 114 (122: 130) has been worked, thus ending with a WS row.
Shape armhole
Keeping chart correct, cast off 4 sts at beg of next row. 39 (41: 44) sts.
Work 1 row, thus ending with a WS row.
Shape front slope
Place marker at beg of last row to denote start of front slope shaping.
Dec 1 st at armhole edge on next 5 rows, then on foll 3 alt rows **and at same time** dec 1 st at front slope edge on next and every foll 4th row. 28 (30: 33) sts.
Dec 1 st at front slope edge **only** on every foll 4th row from previous dec until 18 (20: 23) sts rem.
Work 5 rows, thus ending with chart row 170 (178: 186) and a WS row.
Shape shoulder
Cast off 6 (6: 7) sts at beg of next row, then 6 (7: 8) sts at beg of foll alt row.
Work 1 row.
Cast off rem 6 (7: 8) sts.

RIGHT FRONT
Work as for left front, reversing all shapings and placing pocket as folls:
Place pocket
Next row (RS): Patt 12 (13: 14) sts, slip next 20 sts on a holder, patt across 20 sts of second pocket lining, patt 7 (7: 11) sts, [patt 2 tog] 0 (1: 0) times. 39 (41: 45) sts.

SLEEVES (both alike)
Cast on 33 sts using 4¹/₂mm (US 7) needles and yarn A.
Beg with a K row, work in patt from sleeve chart, shaping sides by inc 1 st at each end of 21st and every foll 8th row until there are 49 sts, then on every foll 10th row until there are 53 sts, taking inc sts into patt.
Cont without further shaping until chart row 104 has been worked, ending with a WS row.
Shape top
Keeping chart correct, cast off 4 sts at beg of next 2 rows. 45 sts.
Dec 1 st at each end of next and foll 2 alt rows, then on every foll 4th row until 31 sts rem.
Work 1 row, thus ending with a WS row.
Dec 1 st at each end of next and foll 2 alt rows. 25 sts.
Dec 1 st at each end of next 5 rows, thus ending with a WS row.
Cast off rem 15 sts.

One colour version
Work as for Two colour version but using one colour throughout.

MAKING UP
PRESS all pieces as described on the information page.
Join both shoulder seams using back stitch.
Button band
With RS facing, using 4mm (US 6) needles and yarn A, pick up and knit 77 (82: 87) sts evenly along left front opening edge between start of front slope shaping and cast on edge.
K 2 rows.
Cast off knitways.
Buttonhole band
With RS facing, using 4mm (US 6) needles and yarn A, pick up and knit 77 (82: 87) sts evenly along right front opening edge

between cast on edge and start of front slope shaping.
K 1 row.

Next row (RS) (buttonhole row): K2, *K2tog, (yfwd) twice (to make a st - drop extra loop on next row), K12 (13: 14), rep from * 4 times more, K2tog, (yfwd) twice (to make a st - drop extra loop on next row), K3.
Cast off knitways.

Left collar
Cast on 3 sts using 4½mm (US 7) needles and yarn A.
K 4 rows, inc 1 st at end of 3rd of these rows. 4 sts.
Now work in fringe patt as folls:

Row 1 (RS): Cast on 4 sts and then cast off same 4 sts - now termed "fringe 1", K1, fringe 1, K1.

Row 2: Inc in first st, K1, P1, K1. 5 sts.

Rows 3 and 4: Knit.

Row 5: (K1, fringe 1) twice, inc in last st. 6 sts.

Row 6: P2, (K1, P1) twice.

Row 7: Knit.

Row 8: Inc in first st, K to end. 7 sts.

Row 9: (Fringe 1, K1) 3 times, K1.

Row 10: P1, (P1, K1) 3 times.

Row 11: K to last st, inc in last st. 8 sts.

Row 12: Knit.

Row 13: (K1, fringe 1) 3 times, K2.

Row 14: Inc in first st, P1, (K1, P1) 3 times. 9 sts.

Rows 15 and 16: Knit.

Row 17: (Fringe 1, K1) 4 times, inc in last st. 10 sts.

Row 18: P3, K1, (P1, K1) 3 times.

Row 19: Knit.

Row 20: Inc in first st, K to end. 11 sts.

Row 21: (K1, fringe 1) 5 times, K1.

Row 22: P1, (K1, P1) 5 times.
These 22 rows set position of patt and start to shape inner edge.
Keeping patt correct as now set, inc 1 st at end of next row and **at same edge** on every foll 3rd row until there are 26 sts, taking inc sts into patt.
Patt a further 21 rows, thus ending after a WS row after a fringe row.
Cast off.

Right collar
Cast on 3 sts using 4½mm (US 7) needles and yarn A.
K 4 rows, inc 1 st at beg of 3rd of these rows. 4 sts.
Now work in fringe patt as folls:

Row 1 (RS): (K1, fringe 1) twice.

Row 2: K1, P1, K1, inc in last st. 5 sts.

Rows 3 and 4: Knit.

Row 5: Inc in first st, (fringe 1, K1) twice. 6 sts.

Row 6: (P1, K1) twice, P2.

Row 7: Knit.

Row 8: K5, inc in last st. 7 sts.

Row 9: K1, (K1, fringe 1) 3 times.

Row 10: (K1, P1) 3 times, P1.

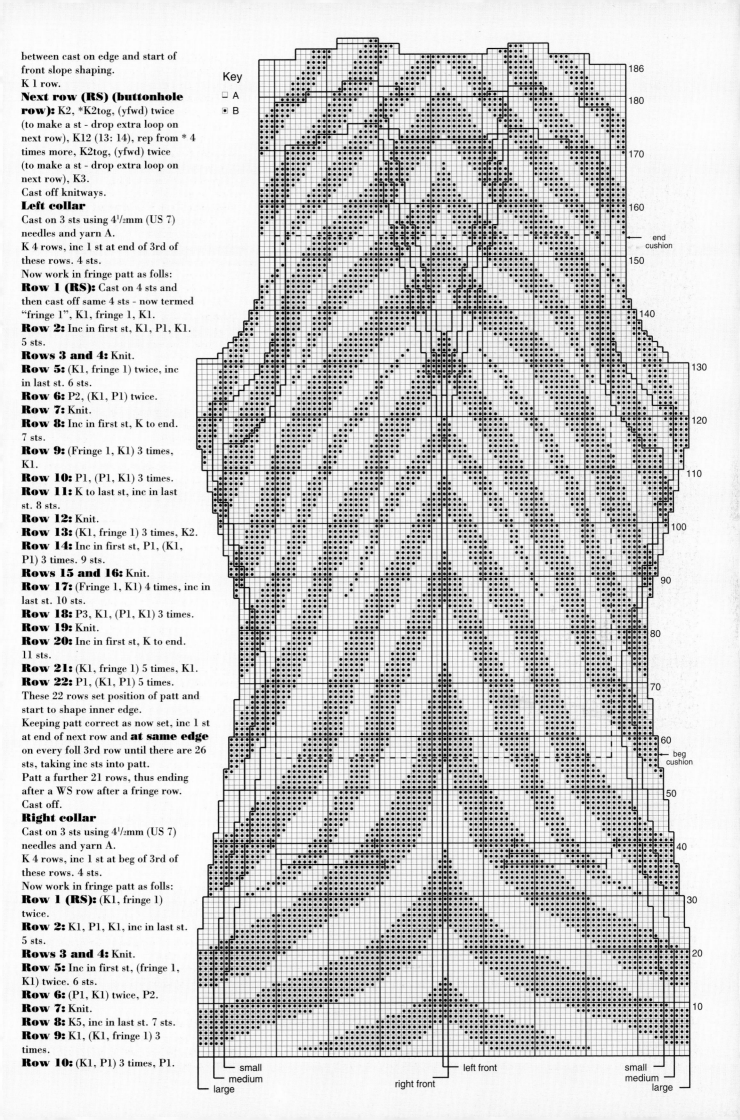

Key
☐ A
⊡ B

186
180
170
160
← end cushion
150
140
130
120
110
100
90
80
70
60
← beg cushion
50
40
30
20
10

small medium large — left front
right front — small medium large

Row 11: Inc in first st, K6. 8 sts.
Row 12: Knit.
Row 13: K2, (fringe 1, K1) 3 times.
Row 14: (P1, K1) 3 times, P1, inc in last st. 9 sts.
Rows 15 and 16: Knit.
Row 17: Inc in first st, (K1, fringe 1) 4 times. 10 sts.
Row 18: (K1, P1) 3 times, K1, P3.
Row 19: Knit.
Row 20: K9, inc in last st. 11 sts.
Row 21: (K1, fringe 1) 5 times, K1.
Row 22: P1, (K1, P1) 5 times.
Complete to match left collar, reversing shapings.
Join cast off edges of collar pieces. Sew collar to neck edge, matching cast on edges to top of button and buttonhole bands and collar seam to centre back neck.

Pocket tops
Slip 20 pocket sts onto 4mm (US 6) needles and rejoin yarn A with RS facing.
K 3 rows, ending with a RS row.
Cast off knitways.

Belt
Cast on 230 sts using 4mm (US 6) needles and yarn A.
K 10 rows.
Cast off loosely and evenly knitways.

Cuffs
Cast on 33 sts using 4½mm (US 7) needles and yarn A.
K 4 rows.
Now work in fringe patt as folls:
Row 1 (RS): *K1, fringe 1, rep from * to last st, K1.
Row 2: P1, *K1, P1, rep from * to end.
Rows 3 and 4: Knit.
Row 5: K2, *fringe 1, K1, rep from * to last st, K1.
Row 6: P2, *K1, P1, rep from * to last st, P1.
Rows 7 and 8: Knit.
Rep the last 8 rows twice more.
K 2 rows.
Cast off knitways.
Join row ends of cuff to form ring. With RS of cuff to WS of sleeve, sew cuff to sleeve cast on edge.
Fold cuff back to RS.
See information page for finishing instructions.

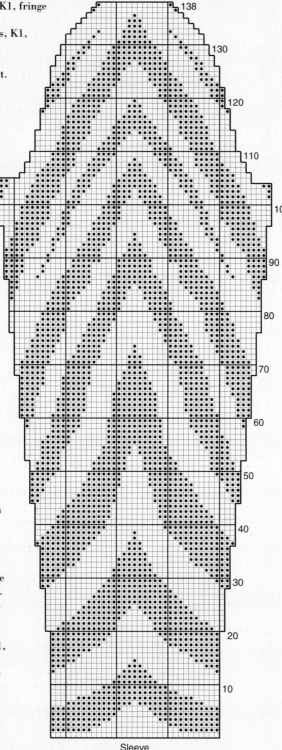

Sleeve

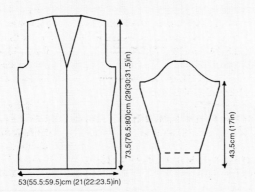

53(55.5:59.5)cm (21(22:23.5)in)

73.5(76.5:80)cm (29(30:31.5)in)

43.5cm (17in)

Reef

KIM HARGREAVES

YARNS
Rowan Chunky Chenille
childrens

4-6	6-8	8-9	9-11	12-14yrs
5	6	6	7	8 x 100gm

(Photographed in 380 Maple)

ladies			mens		
S	M	L	M	L	XL
9	10	10	9	9	10 x100gm

(Mens photographed in both 348 Elephant & 363 French Mustard)

NEEDLES
1 pair 4mm (no 8) (US 6) needles
1 pair 4½mm (no 7) (US 7) needles

TENSION
16 sts and 24 rows to 10 cm measured over stocking stitch using 4½mm (US 7) needles.

Pattern note: The pattern is written for the five childrens sizes, followed by the ladies sizes in **bold**, followed by the mens sizes.

BACK

Cast on 74 (78: 82: 86: 90: **94: 98: 102:** 102: 106: 110) sts using 4mm (US 6) needles.
Beg with a K row, work 8 (8: 8: 8: 8: **10: 10: 10:** 10: 10: 10) rows in st st to form roll.
Change to 4¹/₂mm (US 7) needles.
Now work in either st st (beg with a K row) or **reversed** st st (beg with a P row) until back measures 29.5 (32.5: 35: 37: 39: **43.5: 46: 49:** 43.5: 46: 49) cm, ending with a WS row.

Shape armholes
Childrens sizes only
Cast off 4 sts at beg of next 2 rows. 66 (70: 74: 78: 82) sts.

Adult sizes only
Cast off 4 sts at beg of next 2 rows. (**86: 90: 94:** 94: 98: 102) sts.
Dec 1 st at each end of next 4 rows. (**78: 82: 86:** 86: 90: 94) sts.

All sizes
Cont without further shaping until armholes measures 20 (21: 22: 23: 24: **25: 25: 25:** 25: 25: 25) cm, ending with a WS row.

Crew neck version only
Shape back neck and shoulders
Cast off 7 (7: 8: 8: 9: **8: 9: 9:** 9: 10: 10) sts at beg of next 2 rows. 52 (56: 58: 62: 64: **62: 64: 68:** 68: 70: 74) sts.
Next row (RS): Cast off 7 (7: 8: 8: 9: **8: 9: 9:** 9: 10: 10) sts, patt until there are 11 (12: 11: 13: 13: **12: 12: 14:** 13: 13: 15) sts on right needle and turn, leaving rem sts on a holder.
Work each side of neck separately.
Cast off 4 sts at beg of row.
Cast off rem 7 (8: 7: 9: 9: **8: 8: 10:** 9: 9: 11) sts.
With RS facing, rejoin yarn to rem sts, cast off centre 16 (18: 20: 20: 20: **22: 22: 22:** 24: 24: 24) sts, patt to end.
Work to match first side, reversing shapings.

V neck and collared versions only
Shape back neck and shoulders
Cast off 7 (8: 8: 9: 9: **8: 9: 10:** 9: 10: 11) sts at beg of next 2 rows. 52 (54: 58: 60: 64: **62: 64: 66:** 68: 70: 72) sts.
Next row (RS): Cast off 7 (8: 8: 9: 9: **8: 9: 10:** 9: 10: 11) sts, patt until there are 12 (11: 12: 12: 14: **13: 13: 13:** 14: 14: 14) sts on right needle and turn, leaving rem sts on a holder.
Work each side of neck separately.
Cast off 4 sts at beg of row.
Cast off rem 8 (7: 8: 8: 10: **9: 9: 9:** 10: 10: 10) sts.
With RS facing, rejoin yarn to rem sts, cast off centre 14 (16: 18: 18: 18: **20: 20: 20:** 22: 22: 22) sts, patt to end.
Work to match first side, reversing shapings.

FRONT
Crew neck version only
Work as for back until 14 (14: 16: 16: 16: **18: 18: 18:** 18: 18: 18) rows less have been worked before start of shoulder shaping, thus ending with a WS row.
Shape neck
Next row (RS): Patt 31 (32: 34: 36: 38: **35: 37: 39:** 38: 40: 42) and turn, leaving rem sts on a holder.
Work each side of neck separately.

Cast off 4 sts at beg of next row. 27 (28: 30: 32: 34: **31: 33: 35:** 34: 36: 38) sts.
Dec 1 st at neck edge on next 3 rows, then on every foll alt row until 21 (22: 23: 25: 27: **25: 27: 29:** 28: 30: 32) sts rem.

Adult sizes only
Dec 1 st at neck edge on 4th row from previous dec. (**24: 26: 28:** 27: 29: 31) sts.

All sizes
Work 3 rows, thus ending with a WS row.
Shape shoulder
Cast off 7 (7: 8: 8: 9: **8: 9: 9:** 9: 10: 10) sts at beg of next and foll alt row. Work 1 row.
Cast off rem 7 (8: 7: 9: 9: **8: 8: 10:** 9: 9: 11) sts.
With RS facing, rejoin yarn to rem sts, cast off centre 4 (6: 6: 6: 6: **8: 8: 8:** 10: 10: 10) sts, patt to end.
Work to match first side, reversing shapings.

V neck version only
Work as for back until 32 (34: 34: 36: 36: **38: 38: 38:** 38: 38: 38) rows less have been worked before start of shoulder shaping, thus ending with a WS row.
Divide for front neck
Next row (RS): Patt 33 (35: 37: 39: 41: **39: 41: 43:** 43: 45: 47) and turn, leaving rem sts on a holder.
Work each side of neck separately.
Work 1 row.
Dec 1 st at neck edge on next and every foll alt row to 25 (26: 26: 29: 31: **28: 30: 32:** 30: 32: 34) sts, then on every foll 4th row from previous dec until 22 (23: 24: 26: 28: **25: 27: 29:** 28: 30: 32) sts rem.
Work 3 rows, thus ending with a WS row.
Shape shoulder
Cast off 7 (8: 8: 9: 9: **8: 9: 10:** 9: 10: 11) sts at beg of next and foll alt row.
Work 1 row.
Cast off rem 8 (7: 8: 8: 10: **9: 9: 9:** 10: 10: 10) sts.
With RS facing, rejoin yarn to rem sts, patt to end.
Work to match first side, reversing shapings.

Collared version only
Work as for back until 28 (28: 32: 32: 32: **36: 36: 36:** 36: 36: 36) rows less have been worked before start of shoulder shaping, thus ending with a WS row.
Divide for front opening
Next row (RS): Patt 30 (32: 34: 36: 38: **36: 38: 40:** 40: 42: 44) and turn, leaving rem sts on a holder.
Work each side of neck separately.
Work 12 (12: 14: 14: 14: **16: 16: 16:** 16: 16) rows, thus ending with a RS row.
Shape neck
Cast off 3 (3: 3: 3: 3: **4: 4: 4:** 5: 5: 5) sts at beg of next row. 27 (29: 31: 33: 35: **32: 34: 36:** 35: 37: 39) sts.
Dec 1 st at neck edge on next 3 (3: 5: 5: 5: **5: 5: 5:** 5: 5: 5) rows, then on every foll alt row until 22 (23: 24: 26: 28: **25: 27: 29:** 28: 30: 32) sts rem.
Work 7 (5: 7: 7: 7: **9: 9: 9:** 9: 9: 9) rows, thus ending with a WS row.
Shape shoulder
Cast off 7 (8: 8: 9: 9: **8: 9: 10:** 9: 10: 11) sts at beg of next and foll alt row.
Work 1 row.
Cast off rem 8 (7: 8: 8: 10: **9: 9: 9:** 10: 10: 10) sts.

With RS facing, slip centre 6 sts on a safety pin, rejoin yarn to rem sts, patt to end.
Work to match first side, reversing shapings.

SLEEVES (both alike)
Cast on 36 (36: 40: 40: 40: **48: 48: 48:** 52: 52: 52) sts using 4mm (US 6) needles.
Beg with a K row, work 8 (8: 8: 8: 8: **10: 10: 10:** 10: 10: 10) rows in st st to form roll.
Change to 4¹/₂mm (US 7) needles.
Now work in either st st (beg with a K row) or **reversed** st st (beg with a P row), shaping sides by inc 1 st at each end of next row and every foll 4th (4th: 4th: 4th: 4th: **6th: 6th: 6th:** 8th: 8th: 8th) row to 58 (52: 44: 50: 50: **72: 72: 72:** 76: 76: 76) sts, then on every foll 6th (6th: 6th: 6th: 6th: **8th: 8th: 8th:** 10th: 10th: 10th) row (from previous inc) until there are 64 (68: 70: 74: 76: **80: 80: 80:** 80: 80: 80) sts.
Cont without further shaping until sleeve measures 33 (38: 40.5: 43: 45.5: **48: 48: 48:** 53: 53: 53) cm, ending with a WS row.
Shape top
Childrens sizes
Cast off loosely and evenly.
Adults sizes
Cast off 4 sts at beg of next 2 rows.
Dec 1 st at each end of next 4 rows.
Cast off rem 64 sts loosely and evenly.

MAKING UP
PRESS all pieces as described on the information page.

Crew neck version only
Join right shoulder seam using back stitch.
Neckband
With RS facing and using 4mm (US 6) needles, pick up and knit 12 (12: 13: 13: 13: **14: 14: 14:** 14: 14: 14) sts down left front neck, 12 (14: 14: 14: 14: **16: 16: 16:** 18: 18: 18) sts across centre front, 12 (12: 13: 13: 13: **14: 14: 14:** 14: 14: 14) sts up right front neck and 24 (26: 28: 28: 28: **30: 30: 30:** 32: 32: 32) sts across back neck. 60 (64: 68: 68: 68: **74: 74: 74:** 78: 78: 78) sts.
Beg with a P row, work 8 (8: 10: 10: 10: **12: 12: 12:** 12: 12: 12) rows in st st.
Cast off loosely and evenly.
See information page for finishing instructions.

V neck version only
Join right shoulder seam using back stitch.
Neckband
With RS facing and using 4mm (US 6) needles, pick up and knit 29 (31: 31: 33: 33: **35: 35: 35:** 35: 35: 35) sts down left front neck, 29 (31: 31: 33: 33: **35: 35: 35:** 35: 35: 35) sts up right front neck and 22 (24: 26: 26: 26: **28: 28: 28:** 30: 30: 30) sts across back neck. 80 (86: 88: 92: 92: **98: 98: 98:** 100: 100: 100) sts.
Beg with a P row, work 5 rows in st st.
Cast off loosely and evenly.
See information page for finishing instructions.

Collared version only
Join shoulder seams using back stitch.
Left front band
Girls or ladies version
Cast on 7 sts using 4mm (US 6) needles.
Row 1 (RS): K2, P1, K1, P1, K2.

Boys or mens version

Slip 6 sts left on safety pin at base of front opening onto 4mm (US 6) needles and rejoin yarn with RS facing.
Row 1 (RS): K2, P1, inc in next st, K2. 7 sts.

Both versions

Row 2 (WS): (K1, P1) 3 times, K1.
Row 3: K2, P1, K1, P1, K2.
Rep last 2 rows until band, when slightly stretched, fits up left front opening edge to neck shaping, ending with a WS row.
Break yarn and leave sts on a safety pin.
Slip stitch band in place.

Right front band
Girls or ladies version

Slip 6 sts left on safety pin at base of front opening onto 4mm (US 6) needles and rejoin yarn with RS facing.
Row 1 (RS): K2, P1, inc in next st, K2. 7 sts.

Boys or mens version

Cast on 7 sts using 4mm (US 6) needles.
Row 1 (RS): K2, P1, K1, P1, K2.

Both versions

Complete as left front band, but do NOT break off yarn.
Slip stitch band in place to right front opening edge, sewing cast on edge of one band in place behind other band.

Collar

With RS facing and using 4mm (US 6) needles, rib across 7 sts of right front band as folls: K2, (P1, K1) twice, P1, pick up and knit 15 (15: 17: 17: 17: **20: 20: 20:** 21: 21: 21) sts up right front neck, 23 (25: 27: 27: 27: **29: 29: 29:** 31: 31: 31) sts across back neck, and 15 (15: 17: 17: 17: **20: 20: 20:** 21: 21: 21) sts down left front neck, then rib across 7 sts of left front band left on safety pin as folls: (P1, K1) 3 times, K1. 67 (69: 75: 75: 75: **83: 83: 83:** 87: 87: 87) sts.
Working first and last st of every row as a K st, work 8 (8: 8: 8: 8: **10: 10: 10:** 12: 12: 12) cm in rib as set by bands.
Cast off loosely and evenly in rib.
See information page for finishing instructions.

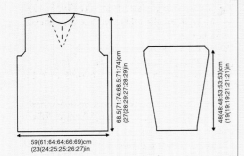

59(61:64:64:66:69)cm
(23(24:25:25:26:27)in

68.5(71:74:68.5:71:74)cm
(27(28:29:27:28:29)in

48(48:48:53:53:53)cm
(19(19:19:21:21:21)in

child

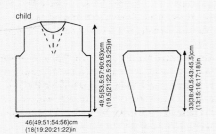

46(49:51:54:56)cm
(18(19:20:21:22)in

49.5(53.5:57:60:63)cm
(19.5(21:22.5:23.5:25)in

33(38:40.5:43:45.5)cm
(13:15:16:17:18)in

Design number 3

Hawk

KIM HARGREAVES

YARNS

Rowan Chunky Chenille

	ladies		mens		
S	M	L	M	L	XL
5	6	6	8	8	9 x100gm

(Ladies photographed in 381 Blackcurrant, mens in 362 Forest Green)

NEEDLES

1 pair 4mm (no 8) (US 6) needles
1 pair 4¹/₂mm (no 7) (US 7) needles 3.75m

TENSION

16 sts and 24 rows to 10 cm measured over rib patt using 4¹/₂mm (US 7) needles.

Pattern note: The pattern is written for the ladies sizes, followed by the mens sizes in **bold**.

BACK
Cast on 64 (68: 72: **98: 102: 106**) sts using 4mm (US 8) needles. should be US6?
Row 1 (RS): P0 (1: 3: **4: 6: 0**), K5 (6: 6:

6: **6: 2**), *P6, K6, rep from * to last 11 (1: 3: **4: 6: 8**) sts, P6 (1: 3: **4: 6: 6**), K5 (0: 0: **0: 0: 2**).
Row 2: K0 (1: 3: **4: 6: 0**), P5 (6: 6: **6: 6: 2**), *K6, P6, rep from * to last 11 (1: 3: **4: 6: 8**) sts, K6 (1: 3: **4: 6: 6**), P5 (0: 0: **0: 0: 2**).
These 2 rows form rib patt.
Work a further 6 (8: 10: **8: 8: 8**) rows in patt.
Change to 4¹/₂mm (US 7) needles.

Ladies sizes only

Cont in patt, shaping side seams by inc 1 st at each end of next and every foll 8th (10th: 12th) row until there are 74 (78: 82) sts, taking inc sts into patt.

All sizes

Cont in patt until back measures 26 (28.5: 31: **40: 42.5: 45**) cm, end with a WS row.

Shape armholes

Keeping patt correct, cast off 4 sts at beg of next 2 rows. 66 (70: 74: **90: 94: 98**) sts.
Dec 1 st at each end of next 5 rows, then on every foll alt row until 50 (54: 58: **74: 78: 82**) sts rem.
Cont without further shaping until armhole measures 20 (20: 20: **23.5: 23.5: 23.5**) cm, ending with a WS row.

Shape back neck and shoulders

Cast off 4 (5: 6: **8: 8: 9**) sts at beg of next 2 rows. 42 (44: 46: **58: 62: 64**) sts
Next row (RS): Cast off 4 (5: 6: **8: 8: 9**) sts, patt until there are 9 (9: 9: **11: 13: 13**) sts on right needle and turn, leaving rem sts on a holder.
Work each side of neck separately.
Cast off 4 sts at beg of next row.
Cast off rem 5 (5: 5: **7: 9: 9**) sts.
With RS facing, rejoin yarn to rem sts, cast off centre 16 (16: 16: **20: 20: 20**) sts, patt to end.
Work to match first side, reversing shapings.

FRONT
Work as for back until 18 rows less have been worked before start of shoulder shaping, thus ending with a WS row.

Shape neck

Next row (RS): Patt 20 (22: 24: **33: 35: 37**) and turn, leave rem sts on a holder.
Work each side of neck separately.

Mens sizes only

Cast off 4 sts at beg of next row.
(**29: 31: 33**) sts.

All sizes

Dec 1 st at neck edge on next 4 (4: 4: **3: 3: 3**) rows, then on foll alt row.
15 (17: 19: **25: 27: 29**) sts.
Work 3 rows.
Dec 1 st at neck edge on next and foll 4th row. 13 (15: 17: **23: 25: 27**) sts.
Work 3 rows, thus ending after a WS row.

Shape shoulder

Cast off 4 (5: 6: **8: 8: 9**) sts at beg of next and foll alt row. Work 1 row.
Cast off rem 5 (5: 5: **7: 9: 9**) sts.
With RS facing, rejoin yarn to rem sts, cast off centre 10 (10: 10: **8: 8: 8**) sts, patt to end.
Work to match first side, reversing shapings.

SLEEVES (both alike)
Cast on 32 (32: 32: **40: 40: 40**) sts using 4mm (US 6) needles. 4mm
Row 1 (RS): K1 (1: 1: **5: 5: 5**), *P6, K6, rep from * to last 7 (7: 7: **11: 11: 11**) sts, P6, K1 (1: 1: **5: 5: 5**).

Row 2: P1 (1: 1: **5: 5: 5**), *K6, P6, rep from * to last 7 (7: 7: **11: 11: 11**) sts, K6, P1 (1: 1: **5: 5: 5**).
These 2 rows form rib patt.
Work a further 6 (6: 6: **8: 8: 8**) rows in patt.
Change to 4½mm (US 7) needles.
Cont in patt, shaping sides by inc 1 st at each end of next (next: next: **3rd: 3rd: 3rd**) row and every foll 8th (8th: 8th: **12th: 12th: 12th**) row to 36 (36: 36: **46: 46: 46**) sts, then on every foll 10th (10th: 10th: **14th: 14th: 14th**) row (from previous inc) until there are 52 (52: 52: **56: 56: 56**) sts, taking inc sts into patt.
Cont without further shaping until sleeve measures 43.5 (43.5: 43.5: **48.5: 48.5: 48.5**) cm, ending with a WS row.
Shape top
Keeping patt correct, cast off 4 sts at beg of next 2 rows. 44 (44: 44: **48: 48: 48**) sts.
Dec 1 st at each end of next 3 rows, then on every foll alt row until 34 (34: 34: **38: 38: 38**) sts rem.
Work 3 rows, thus ending with a WS row.
Dec 1 st at each end of next and every foll 4th row until 26 (26: 26: **30: 30: 30**) sts rem.
Work 1 row, thus ending with a WS row.
Dec 1 st at each end of next and foll 2 (2: 2: **3: 3: 3**) rows. 20 (20: 20: **22: 22: 22**) sts.
Dec 1 st at each end of next row, thus ending with a WS row. 18 (18: 18: **20: 20: 20**) sts.
Cast off 4 sts at beg of next 2 rows.
Cast off rem 10 (10: 10: **12: 12: 12**) sts loosely and evenly.

MAKING UP
PRESS all pieces as described on the information page.
Join right shoulder seam using back stitch.
Neckband
With RS facing and using 4mm (US 6) needles, pick up and knit 20 sts down left front neck, 10 (10: 10: **14: 14: 14**) sts across centre front, 20 sts up right front neck and 24 (24: 24: **30: 30: 30**) sts across back neck. 74 (74: 74: **84: 84: 84**) sts.
Row 1 (WS): K4 (4: 4: **0: 0: 0**), *P6, K6, rep from * to last 10 (10: 10: **12: 12: 12**) sts, P6, K4 (4: 4: **6: 6: 6**).
Row 2: P4 (4: 4: **0: 0: 0**), *K6, P6, rep from * to last 10 (10: 10: **12: 12: 12**) sts, K6, P4 (4: 4: **6: 6: 6**).
Rep the last 2 rows until neckband measures 20 cm. Cast off loosely and evenly in rib.
See info page for finishing instructions.

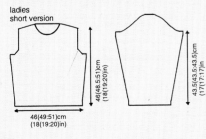

ladies
short version

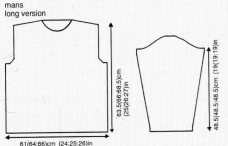

mans
long version

Design number 4

Piper

KIM HARGREAVES

YARNS
Rowan Chunky Chenille

childrens

4-6	6-8	8-9	9-11	12-14yrs	
5	6	6	7	8	x 100gm

(Photographed in 384 Lily)

ladies			mens		
S	M	L	M	L	XL
8	9	9	10	10	11 x 100gm

(Mens photographed in 387 Navy)

NEEDLES
1 pair 3¾mm (no 9) (US 5) needles
1 pair 4½mm (no 7) (US 7) needles

BUTTONS - 8

TENSION
16 sts and 27 rows to 10 cm over ridge pattern, 16 sts and 24 rows to 10 cm measured over stocking stitch using 4½mm (US 7) needles.

Pattern note: The pattern is written for five childrens sizes, followed by the ladies sizes in **bold**, followed by the mens sizes.

BACK
Cast on 73 (77: 81: 85: 89: **85: 89: 93:** 93: 97: 101) sts using 3¾mm (US 5) needles.
Row 1 (RS): Purl.
Row 2: Knit.
Rows 3 and 4: Purl.
Row 5: Knit.
Row 6: Purl.
These 6 rows form ridge patt.
Work a further 10 rows in ridge patt, thus ending with a WS row.
Change to 4½mm (US 7) needles.
Childrens sizes only
Beg with a K row, work in st st until back meas 25 (27: 28: 30: 31) cm, end with WS row.
Adult sizes only
Beg with a K row, now work in st st, shaping side seams by inc 1 st at each end of (**11th: 11th: 11th:** 13th: 13th: 13th) row and every foll (**10th: 10th: 10th:** 12th: 12th: 12th) row until there are (**93: 97: 101:** 101: 105: 109) sts.
Cont without further shaping until back measures (**33: 33: 33:** 42: 42: 42) cm, ending with a WS row.
All sizes
Shape armholes
Keeping patt correct, cast off 4 sts at beg of next 2 rows. 65 (69: 73: 77: 81: **85: 89: 93:** 93: 97: 101) sts.
Adult sizes only
Dec 1 st at each end of next and foll 3 alt rows. (**77: 81: 85:** 85: 89: 93) sts.
All sizes
Work 8 (8: 8: 8: 8: **3: 3: 3:** 5: 5: 5) rows straight, thus ending with a WS row.
Beg with row 1, now work in ridge patt until armholes measure 17 (18: 19: 20: 21: **23: 23: 23:** 25: 25: 25) cm, ending with a WS row.
Shape shoulders and back neck
Cast off 7 (8: 9: 9: 10: **9: 10: 10:** 10: 10: 11) sts at beg of next 2 rows. 51 (53: 55: 59: 61: **59: 61: 65:** 65: 69: 71) sts.
Next row (RS): Cast off 7 (8: 9: 9: 10: **9: 10: 10:** 10: 10: 11) sts, patt until there are 12 (12: 12: 14: 14: **13: 13: 15:** 13: 15: 15) sts on right needle and turn, leaving rem sts on a holder.
Work each side of neck separately.
Cast off 4 sts at beg of next row.
Cast off rem 8 (8: 8: 10: 10: **9: 9: 11:** 9: 11: 11) sts.
With RS facing, rejoin yarn to rem sts, cast off centre 13 (13: 13: 13: 13: **15: 15: 15:** 19: 19: 19) sts, patt to end.
Work to match first side, reversing shapings.

LEFT FRONT
Cast on 41 (43: 45: 47: 49: **47: 49: 51:** 51: 53: 55) sts using 3¾mm (US 5) needles.
Working in ridge patt as for back, proceed as folls:
Boys and mens version only
Work 4 rows, thus ending with a WS row.
Next row (RS) (buttonhole row): K to last 5 sts, K2tog, (yrn) twice (to make a buttonhole - on next row work twice into this hole), K2tog, K1.
Work a further 10 rows, thus ending with a RS row.

Girls and ladies version only

Work 15 rows, thus ending with a RS row.

Both versions

Row 16 (WS): Patt 6 sts and sl these sts onto a safety pin for border, inc in next st, patt to end. 36 (38: 40: 42: 44: **42: 44: 46:** 46: 48: 50) sts.

Change to 4½mm (US 7) needles.

Childrens sizes only

Beg with a K row, work in st st until left front matches back to start of armhole shaping, ending with a WS row.

Adult sizes only

Beg with a K row, now work in st st, shaping side seam by inc 1 st at beg of (**11th: 11th: 11th:** 13th: 13th: 13th) row and every foll (**10th: 10th: 10th:** 12th: 12th: 12th) row until there are (**46: 48: 50:** 50: 52: 54) sts. Cont without further shaping until left front matches back to start of armhole shaping, ending with a WS row.

All sizes

Shape armhole

Keeping patt correct, cast off 4 sts at beg of next row. 32 (34: 36: 38: 40: **42: 44: 46:** 46: 48: 50) sts.

Work 1 row.

Adult sizes only

Dec 1 st at beg of next and foll 3 alt rows. (**38: 40: 42:** 42: 44: 46) sts.

All sizes

Work 8 (8: 8: 8: 8: **3: 3: 3:** 5: 5: 5) rows straight, thus ending with a WS row.

Beg with row 1, now work in ridge patt until 13 (13: 13: 13: 13: **15: 15: 15:** 17: 17: 17) rows less have been worked than on back to start of shoulder shaping, thus ending with a RS row.

Shape neck

Cast off 3 (3: 3: 3: 3: **3: 3: 3:** 4: 4: 4) sts at beg of next row, then 2 (2: 2: 2: 2: **3: 3: 3:** 4: 4: 4) sts at beg of foll alt row. 27 (29: 31: 33: 35: **32: 34: 36:** 34: 36: 38) sts.

Dec 1 st at neck edge on next and foll 4 (4: 4: 4: 4: **3: 3: 3:** 2: 2: 2) alt rows. 22 (24: 26: 28: 30: **28: 30: 32:** 31: 33: 35) sts.

Ladies sizes only

Work 3 rows.

Dec 1 st at neck edge on next row (**27: 29: 31**) sts.

Mens sizes only

Work 3 rows.

Dec 1 st at neck edge on next and foll 4th row. (29: 31: 33) sts.

All sizes

Work 1 row, thus ending with a WS row.

Shape shoulder

Cast off 7 (8: 9: 9: 10: **9: 10: 10:** 10: 10: 11) sts at beg of next and foll alt row. Work 1 row. Cast off rem 8 (8: 8: 10: 10: **9: 9: 11:** 9: 11: 11) sts.

RIGHT FRONT

Cast on 41 (43: 45: 47: 49: **47: 49: 51:** 51: 53: 55) sts using 3¾mm (US 5) needles.

Working in ridge patt as for back, proceed as folls:

Girls and ladies version only

Work 4 rows, thus ending with a WS row.

Next row (RS) (buttonhole row):
K1, K2tog, (yrn) twice (to make a buttonhole - on next row work twice into this hole), K2tog, K to end.

Work a further 10 rows, thus ending with a RS row.

Boys and mens version only

Work 15 rows, thus ending with a RS row.

Both versions

Row 16 (WS): Patt to last 7 sts, inc in next st, turn and leave rem 6 sts on a safety pin for border. 36 (38: 40: 42: 44: **42: 44: 46:** 46: 48: 50) sts.

Change to 4½mm (US 7) needles and complete to match left front, reversing shaping.

LEFT SLEEVE

Front panel

Cast on 30 (30: 31: 31: 31: **32: 32: 32:** 33: 33: 33) sts using 4½mm (US 7) needles.

**Row 1 (RS): P5, K to end.

Row 2: P to last 5 sts, K5.

Row 3: P5, K to last st, inc in last st.

Row 4: Purl.

Row 5: Knit.

Row 6: Purl.

These 6 rows form patt - edge 5 sts in ridge patt with rem sts in st st.

Keeping patt correct, work a further 8 (8: 8: 8: 8: **10: 10: 10:** 12: 12: 12) rows, inc 1 st at end of every foll 4th (6th: 6th: 4th: 4th: **4th: 4th: 4th:** 4th: 4th: 4th) row from previous inc.** 33 (32: 33: 34: 34: **36: 36: 36:** 37: 37: 37) sts.

Break yarn and leave sts on a holder.

Back panel

Cast on 10 (10: 11: 11: 11: **12: 12: 12:** 13: 13: 13) sts using 4½mm (US 7) needles.

***Row 1 (RS): K to last 5 sts, P5.

Row 2: K5, P to end.

These 2 rows set patt - edge 5 sts in ridge patt with rem sts in st st.

Keeping patt correct, work a further 12 (12: 12: 12: 12: **14: 14: 14:** 16: 16: 16) rows, inc 1 st at beg of next and every foll 4th (6th: 6th: 4th: 4th: **4th: 4th: 4th:** 4th: 4th: 4th) row.*** 13 (12: 13: 14: 14: **16: 16: 16:** 17: 17: 17) sts.

Join panels

Next row (RS): [Inc in first st] 0 (1: 1: 0: 0: **0: 0: 0:** 1: 1: 1) times, K to last 5 sts of back panel, with RS facing and holding front panel in front of back panel, K tog next st of back panel with first st of front panel, (K tog next st of each panel) 3 times, K tog last st of back panel with next st of front panel, K to last 0 (1: 1: 0: 0: **0: 0: 0:** 1: 1: 1) st of front panel, [inc in last st] 0 (1: 1: 0: 0: **0: 0: 0:** 1: 1: 1) times. 41 (41: 43: 43: 43: **47: 47: 47:** 51: 51: 51) sts.

****Beg with a P row, now cont in st st, shaping sides by inc 1 st at each end of every foll 6th row (from previous inc) until there are 55 (57: 61: 65: 67: **73: 73: 73:** 81: 81: 81) sts.

Cont without further shaping until sleeve measures 27.5 (32.5: 35: 37.5: 40: **42.5: 42.5: 42.5:** 47.5: 47.5: 47.5) cm, ending with a WS row.

Shape top

Childrens sizes

Cast off loosely and evenly.

Adults sizes

Cast off 4 sts at beg of next 2 rows. (**65: 65: 65:** 73: 73: 73) sts.

Dec 1 st at each end of next and foll 2 alt rows.

Work 1 row.

Cast off rem (**59: 59: 59:** 67: 67: 67) sts loosely and evenly.

RIGHT SLEEVE

Back panel

Cast on 10 (10: 11: 11: 11: **12: 12: 12:** 13: 13: 13) sts using 4½mm (US 7) needles.

Work as for front panel of left sleeve from ** to **. 13 (12: 13: 14: 14: **16: 16: 16:** 17: 17: 17) sts.

Break yarn and leave sts on a holder.

Front panel

Cast on 30 (30: 31: 31: 31: **32: 32: 32:** 33: 33: 33) sts using 4½mm (US 7) needles.

Work as for back panel of left sleeve from *** to ***. 33 (32: 33: 34: 34: **36: 36: 36:** 37: 37: 37) sts.

Join panels

Next row (RS): [Inc in first st] 0 (1: 1: 0: 0: **0: 0: 0:** 1: 1: 1) times, K to last 5 sts of front panel, with RS facing and holding front panel in front of back panel, K tog next st of front panel with first st of back panel, (K tog next st of each panel) 3 times, K tog last st of front panel with next st of back panel, K to last 0 (1: 1: 0: 0: **0: 0: 0:** 1: 1: 1) st of back panel, [inc in last st] 0 (1: 1: 0: 0: **0: 0: 0:** 1: 1: 1) times. 41 (41: 43: 43: 43: **47: 47: 47:** 51: 51: 51) sts.

Complete as for left sleeve from ****.

MAKING UP

PRESS all pieces as described on the information page.

Join shoulder seams using back stitch.

Button border

Boys and mens sizes only

Slip 6 sts left on right front safety pin onto 3¾mm (US 5) needles and rejoin yarn with WS facing.

Girls and ladies sizes only

Slip 6 sts left on left front safety pin onto 3¾mm (US 5) needles and rejoin yarn with RS facing.

All sizes

Cont in ridge patt as set until border, when slightly stretched, fits up front opening edge to neck shaping.

Slip st border in position.

Mark positions for 6 buttons on this band - lowest button level with buttonhole in other front, next button just above lower band, top button 1 cm below neck and rem 3 buttons evenly spaced between.

Buttonhole border

Work to match button border, rejoining yarn with opposite side of work facing and with the addition of a further 5 buttonholes worked to correspond with positions marked for buttons as folls:

Buttonhole row (RS): Patt 1, work 2 tog, (yrn) twice (to make buttonhole - on next row work twice into this hole), work 2 tog, patt 1.

Collar

Cast on 63 (63: 63: 63: 63: **71: 71: 71:** 83: 83: 83) sts using 3¾mm (US 5) needles.

Row 1 (RS): K2, P to last 2 sts, K2.

Row 2: Knit.

Rows 3 and 4: K2, P to last 2 sts, K2.

Row 5: Knit.

Row 6: K2, P to last 2 sts, K2.

These 6 rows form ridge patt with 2 edge sts worked as K sts on every row.

Keeping patt correct, proceed as foll:

Next row (RS) (inc): K2, M1, patt to last 2 sts, M1, K2.

Work 3 rows.

Rep last 4 rows 2 (2: 2: 2: 2: **4: 4: 4:** 4: 4: 4) times more, and then first 3 (3: 3: 3: 3: **1: 1: 1:** 1: 1: 1) of these rows again. 71 (71: 71: 71: 71: **83: 83: 83:** 95: 95: 95) sts

Knit 3 rows, thus ending with a **WS** row.

Cast off loosely knitways.

Sew cast-on edge of collar to neck edge, positioning ends of collar midway across top of front borders.

Left cuff

Cast on 35 (35: 37: 37: 37: **39: 39: 39:** 43: 43: 43) sts using 3³/₄mm (US 5) needles.

Beg with row 1, now work in ridge patt as for back as folls:

Work 7 rows, thus ending with a RS row.

Row 8 (WS) (buttonhole row): K to last 5 sts, K2tog, (yrn) twice (to make buttonhole - on next row work twice into this hole), K2tog, K1.

Work 7 rows.

Cast off.

Right cuff

Work as for left cuff, making buttonhole in row 8 as folls:

Row 8 (WS) (buttonhole row): K1, K2tog, (yrn) twice (to make buttonhole - on next row work twice into this hole), K2tog, K to end.

Sew sleeve seams. Sew cast off edge of cuff to lower edge of sleeve.

See information page for finishing instructions.

adult

58(60.5:63:63:65.5:68)cm
(23(24:25:25:26:27)in

56(56:67:67:67)cm
(22(22:22:26.5:26.5:26.5)in

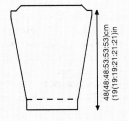

48(48:48:53:53:53)cm
(19(19:19:21:21:21)in

child

45.5(48:50.5:53:55.5)cm
(18(19:20:21:22)in

42(45:47:50:52)cm
(16.5(17.5:18.5:19.5:20.5)in

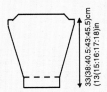

33(38:40.5:43:45.5)cm
(13(15:16:17:18)in

Design number 5

Blade

KIM HARGREAVES

YARNS

Rowan Fine Cotton Chenille

childrens

4-6	6-8	8-9	9-11	12-14yrs
7	7	8	8	9 x 50gm

(Photographed in 409 Plum)

	ladies			mens	
S	M	L	M	L	XL
10	10	11	11	11	12 x 50gm

(Mens photographed in 417 Naval)

NEEDLES

1 pair 2³/₄mm (no 12) (US 2) needles
1 pair 3¹/₄mm (no 10) (US 3) needles

TENSION

25 sts and 36 rows to 10 cm measured over st st using 3¹/₄mm (US 3) needles.

Pattern note: The pattern is written for the five childrens sizes, followed by the ladies sizes in **bold**, followed by the mens sizes.

BACK

Cast on 108 (114: 120: 126: 132: **140: 146: 152:** 152: 158: 164) sts using 2³/₄mm (US 2) needles.

Beg with a K row, work 8 (8: 8: 8: 8: **10: 10: 10:** 10: 10: 10) rows in st st to form roll.

Place markers at both ends of last row.

Change to 3¹/₄mm (US 3) needles and cont in st st until back measures 21 (24: 26.5: 28.5: 30.5: **34: 36: 36:** 36: 38.5: 41) cm from markers, ending with a WS row.

Shape armholes

Cast off 4 sts at beg of next 2 rows.

100 (106: 112: 118: 124: **132: 138: 144:** 144: 150: 156) sts.

Dec 1 st at each end of next 6 (6: 6: 6: 6: **8: 8: 8:** 8: 8: 8) rows. 88 (94: 100: 106: 112: **116: 122: 128:** 128: 134: 140) sts.

Cont without further shaping until armholes measure 19.5 (20.5: 21.5: 22.5: 23.5: **25: 25: 25:** 25: 25: 25) cm, end with a WS row.

Shape shoulders and back neck

Cast off 8 (9: 10: 10: 11: **11: 12: 13:** 13: 14: 15) sts at beg of next 2 rows. 72 (76: 80: 86: 90: **94: 98: 102:** 102: 106: 110) sts.

Next row (RS): Cast off 8 (9: 10: 10: 11: **11: 12: 13:** 13: 14: 15) sts, K until there are 12 (12: 13: 15: 15: **16: 17: 18:** 17: 18: 19) sts on right needle and turn, leaving rem sts on a holder.

Work each side of neck separately.

Cast off 4 sts at beg of next row.

Cast off rem 8 (8: 9: 11: 11: **12: 13: 14:** 13: 14: 15) sts.

With RS facing, rejoin yarn to rem sts, cast off centre 32 (34: 34: 36: 38: **40: 40: 40:** 42: 42: 42) sts, K to end.

Work to match first side, reversing shapings.

FRONT

Work as for back until 16 (16: 16: 16: 16: **22: 22: 22:** 26: 26: 26) rows less have been worked before start of shoulder shaping, thus ending with a WS row.

Shape neck

Next row (RS): K35 (37: 40: 42: 44: **51: 54: 57:** 57: 60: 63) and turn, leave rem sts on a holder.

Work each side of neck separately.

Childrens sizes only

Cast off 4 sts at beg of next row.

31 (33: 36: 38: 40) sts.

Adults sizes only

Cast off 4 sts at beg of next and foll alt row.

(**43: 46: 49:** 49: 52: 55) sts.

All sizes

Dec 1 st at neck edge on next 5 rows, then on foll 2 (2: 2: 2: 2: **4: 4: 4:** 4: 4: 4) alt rows.

24 (26: 29: 31: 33: **34: 37: 40:** 40: 43: 46) sts.

Mens sizes only

Work 3 rows.

Dec 1 st at neck edge on next row.

(39: 42: 45) sts.

All sizes

Work 5 rows, thus ending with a WS row.

Shape shoulder

Cast off 8 (9: 10: 10: 11: **11: 12: 13:** 13: 14: 15) sts at beg of next and foll alt row.

Work 1 row.

Cast off rem 8 (8: 9: 11: 11: **12: 13: 14:** 13: 14: 15) sts.

With RS facing, rejoin yarn to rem sts, cast off centre 18 (20: 20: 22: 24: **14: 14: 14:** 14: 14: 14) sts, K to end.

Work to match first side, reversing shapings.

SLEEVES (both alike)

Cast on 54 (54: 54: 58: 58: **64: 64: 64:** 70: 70: 70) sts using 2³/₄mm (US 2) needles.

Beg with a K row, work 8 (8: 8: 8: 8: **10: 10: 10:** 10: 10: 10) rows in st st to form roll. Place markers at both ends of last row. Change to 3¹/₄mm (US 3) needles and cont in st st, shaping sides by inc 1 st at each end of 3rd and every foll 4th (4th: 4th: 4th: 4th: **4th: 4th: 4th:** 6th: 6th: 6th) row until there are 60 (64: 76: 72: 84: **88: 88: 88:** 126: 126: 126) sts.

Childrens and ladies sizes only

Inc 1 st at each end of every foll 6th row (from previous inc) until there are 98 (102: 108: 112: 118: **126: 126: 126**) sts.

All sizes

Cont without further shaping until sleeve measures 40 (42: 44: 46: 48: **50: 50: 50:** 52: 52: 52) cm from markers, ending with a WS row.

Shape top

Cast off 4 sts at beg of next 2 rows.
90 (94: 100: 104: 110: **118: 118: 118:** 118: 118: 118) sts.
Dec 1 st at each end of next 6 (6: 6: 6: 6: **8: 8: 8:** 8: 8: 8) rows.
Cast off rem 78 (82: 88: 92: 98: **102: 102: 102:** 102: 102: 102) sts loosely and evenly.

MAKING UP

PRESS all pieces as described on the information page.

Join right shoulder seam using back stitch.

Neckband

With RS facing and using 2³/₄mm (US 2) needles, pick up and knit 14 (14: 16: 18: 18: **26: 26: 26:** 30: 30: 30) sts down left front neck, 18 (20: 20: 22: 24: **14: 14: 14:** 14: 14: 14) sts across centre front, 14 (14: 16: 18: 18: **26: 26: 26:** 30: 30: 30) sts up right front neck and 40 (42: 42: 44: 46: **48: 48: 48:** 50: 50: 50) sts across back neck.
86 (90: 94: 102: 106: **114: 114: 114:** 124: 124: 124) sts.
Starting with a P row, work 5 (5: 5: 5: 5: **7.5: 7.5: 7.5:** 7.5: 7.5: 7.5) cm in st st.
Cast off loosely and evenly.
See info page for finishing instructions.

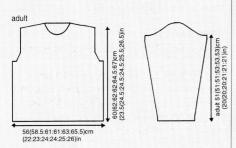

adult

60(62:62:64.5:67)cm
(23.5(24.5:24.5:25.5:26.5)in

56(58.5:61:61:63:65.5)cm
(22:23:24:24:25:26)in

adult 51(51:51:53:53.53)cm
(20(20:20:21:21:21)in

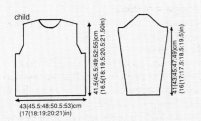

child

41.5(45.5:49.5:49.55)cm
(16.5(18:19.5:20.5:21.50)in

43(45.5:48:50.5:53)cm
(17(18:19:20:21)in

41(43:45:47:49)cm
(16(17:17.5:18.5:19.5)in

Design number 6 🧶🧶

Florence

KIM HARGREAVES

YARNS

Rowan Fine Cotton Chenille

	S	M	L	
High neck version	8	9	9	x 50gm
V neck version	8	9	9	x 50gm

(High neck version photographed in 410 Privet, V neck version in 415 Parched)

NEEDLES

1 pair 3mm (no 11) (US 2/3) needles

High neck version only - 1 pair 2³/₄mm (no 12) (US 2) needles

BUTTONS - 13 for high neck version, or 11 for V neck version

TENSION

24 sts and 36 rows to 10 cm measured over moss st using 3mm (US 2/3) needles.

SPECIAL ABBREVIATION

M2 = Make 2 sts as follows: pick up horizontal loop lying between needles onto left needle and K then P into back of it.

High neck version

BACK

Left back panel

Cast on 23 (25: 27) sts using 3mm (US 2/3) needles.

Row 1 (RS): K1, *P1, K1, rep from * to end. This row forms moss st.
Work a further 7 rows in moss st.
Row 9 (RS) (inc): K1, P1, M2, patt to end. 25 (27: 29) sts.
Patt 7 rows.
Row 17 (RS) (inc): As row 9.
27 (29: 31) sts.
Patt 3 rows, thus ending with a WS row.
Break yarn and leave sts on a holder.

Centre back panel

Cast on 51 (53: 55) sts using 3mm (US 2/3) needles.
Work 8 rows in moss st as for left back panel.
Row 9 (RS) (inc): K1, P1, M2, patt to last 2 sts, M2, P1, K1. 55 (57: 59) sts.
Patt 7 rows.
Row 17 (RS) (inc): As row 9.
59 (61: 63) sts.
Patt 3 rows, thus ending with a WS row.
Break yarn and leave sts on a holder.

Right back panel

Cast on 23 (25: 27) sts using 3mm (US 2/3) needles.
Work 8 rows in moss st as for left back panel.
Row 9 (RS) (inc): Patt to last 2 sts, M2, P1, K1. 25 (27: 29) sts.
Patt 7 rows.
Row 17 (RS) (inc): As row 9.
27 (29: 31) sts.
Patt 3 rows, thus ending with a WS row.

Join panels

Row 21 (RS): Patt first 26 (28: 30) sts of right back panel, with RS facing and holding centre back panel in front of right back panel, K tog last st of right back panel with first st of centre back panel, patt next 57 (59: 61) sts of centre back panel, with RS facing and holding centre back panel in front of left back panel, K tog last st of centre back panel with first st of left back panel, patt rem 26 (28: 30) sts of left back panel.
111 (117: 123) sts.
Patt 1 row, placing markers on 26th (28th: 30th) sts in from each end of row.

Shape side seams and darts

Row 23 (RS) (dec): Patt 2 tog, *patt to within 3 sts of marked st, patt 3 tog, patt marked st, patt 3 tog, rep from * once more, patt to last 2 sts, patt 2 tog. 101 (107: 113) sts.
Patt 19 rows.
Rep last 20 rows twice more. 81 (87: 93) sts.
Row 83 (RS) (inc): Inc in first st, *patt to marked st, M2, patt marked st, M2, rep from * once more, patt to last st, inc in last st. 91 (97: 103) sts.
Patt 19 rows. Rep last 20 rows once more and then row 83 again. 111 (117: 123) sts.
Cont without further shaping until back measures 40.5 cm, ending with a WS row.

Shape armholes

Keeping patt correct, cast off 4 (6: 8) sts at beg of next 2 rows. 103 (105: 107) sts.
Dec 1 st at each end of next 7 rows, then on foll 4 alt rows. 81 (83: 85) sts.
Cont without further shaping until armholes measures 20 cm, ending with a WS row.

Shape shoulders and back neck

Cast off 8 sts at beg of next 2 rows.
65 (67: 69) sts.

Next row (RS): Cast off 8 sts, patt until there are 12 sts on right needle and turn, leaving rem sts on a holder.
Work each side of neck separately.
Cast off 4 sts at beg of next row.
Cast off rem 8 sts.
With RS facing, rejoin yarn to rem sts, cast off centre 25 (27: 29) sts, patt to end.
Work to match first side, reversing shapings.

LEFT FRONT
Left centre panel
Cast on 30 (32: 34) sts using 3mm (US 2/3) needles.
Row 1 (RS): *K1, P1, rep from * to end.
This row sets position of moss st as for back.
Work a further 7 rows in moss st as now set.
Row 9 (RS) (inc): K1, P1, M2, patt to end. 32 (34: 36) sts.
Patt 7 rows.
Row 17 (RS) (inc): As row 9.
34 (36: 38) sts.
Patt 3 rows, thus ending with a WS row.
Break yarn and leave sts on a holder.
Left side panel
Work as for right back panel. 27 (29: 31) sts.
Join panels
Row 21 (RS): Patt first 26 (28: 30) sts of left side panel, with RS facing and holding left centre panel in front of left side panel, K tog last st of left side panel with first st of left centre panel, patt rem 33 (35: 37) sts of left centre panel. 60 (64: 68) sts.
Patt 1 row, placing marker on 26th (28th: 30th) st in from side edge.
Shape side seam and dart
Row 23 (RS) (dec): Patt 2 tog, patt to within 3 sts of marked st, patt 3 tog, patt marked st, patt 3 tog, patt to end.
55 (59: 63) sts.
Patt 19 rows.
Rep last 20 rows twice more. 45 (49: 53) sts.
Row 83 (RS) (inc): Inc in first st, patt to marked st, M2, patt marked st, M2, patt to end. 50 (54: 58) sts.
Patt 19 rows. Rep last 20 rows once more and then row 83 again. 60 (64: 68) sts.***
Cont without further shaping until left front matches back to start of armhole shaping, ending with a WS row.
Shape armhole
Keeping patt correct, cast off 4 (6: 8) sts at beg of next row. 56 (58: 60) sts.
Work 1 row.
Dec 1 st at armhole edge on next 7 rows, then on foll 4 alt rows. 45 (47: 49) sts.
Cont without further shaping until 25 rows less have been worked than on back to start of shoulder shaping, ending with a RS row.
Shape neck
Keeping patt correct, cast off 8 (10: 12) sts at beg of next row and 4 sts at beg of foll alt row. 33 sts.
Dec 1 st at neck edge on next 5 rows, then on foll 2 alt rows. 26 sts.
Work 3 rows. Dec 1 st at neck edge on next and foll 4th row. 24 sts.
Work 5 rows, thus ending at armhole edge.
Shape shoulder
Cast off 8 sts at beg of next and foll alt row. Work 1 row. Cast off rem 8 sts.
Mark positions for 9 buttons on this front - lowest button to be 9 rows above cast on edge, top button to be 4 rows below neck edge and rem 7 evenly spaced between.

RIGHT FRONT
Right side panel
Work as for left back panel. 27 (29: 31) sts.
Right centre panel
Cast on 30 (32: 34) sts using 3mm (US 2/3) needles.
Row 1 (RS): *P1, K1, rep from * to end.
This row sets position of moss st as for back.
Work a further 7 rows in moss st as now set.
Row 9 (RS) (inc) (buttonhole row): P1, K1, P2tog, (yrn) twice (buttonhole made - drop extra loop on next row), patt to last 2 sts, M2, P1, K1.
32 (34: 36) sts.
Note: From this point on, work buttonholes in right front to correspond with positions marked for buttons on left front, working buttonholes as set by last row. No further reference will be made to buttonholes.
Patt 7 rows.
Row 17 (RS) (inc): Patt to last 2 sts, M2, P1, K1. 34 (36: 38) sts.
Patt 3 rows, thus ending with a WS row.
Join panels
Row 21 (RS): Patt first 33 (35: 37) sts of right centre panel, with RS facing and holding right centre panel in front of right side panel, K tog last st of right centre panel with first st of right side panel, patt rem 26 (28: 30) sts of right side panel. 60 (64: 68) sts.
Patt 1 row, placing marker on 26th (28th: 30th) st in from side edge.
Shape side seam and dart
Row 23 (RS) (dec): Patt to within 3 sts of marked st, patt 3 tog, patt marked st, patt 3 tog, patt to last 2 sts, patt 2 tog.
55 (59: 63) sts.
Patt 19 rows.
Rep last 20 rows twice more. 45 (49: 53) sts.
Row 83 (RS) (inc): Patt to marked st, M2, patt marked st, M2, patt to last st, inc in last st. 50 (54: 58) sts.
Patt 19 rows. Rep last 20 rows once more and then row 83 again. 60 (64: 68) sts.****
Complete to match left front, rev shapings.

LEFT SLEEVE
Front panel
Cast on 40 sts using 3mm (US 2/3) needles.
Row 1 (RS): *K1, P1, rep from * to end.
This row sets position of moss st as for back.
Work 25 rows more in moss st as now set, inc 1 st at end of 8th (8th: 6th) of these rows and every foll 8th (8th: 6th) row. 43 (43: 44) sts.
Break yarn and leave sts on a holder.
Back panel
Cast on 14 sts using 3mm (US 2/3) needles.
Row 1 (RS): *P1, K1, rep from * to end.
This row sets position of moss st as for back.
Work 25 rows more in moss st as now set, inc 1 st at beg of 8th (8th: 6th) of these rows and every foll 8th (8th: 6th) row. 17 (17: 18) sts.
Join panels
Row 27 (RS): Patt first 12 (12: 13) sts of back panel, with RS facing and holding front panel in front of back panel, patt tog next st of back panel with first st of front panel, (patt tog next st of each panel) 3 times, patt tog last st of back panel with next st of front panel, patt rem 38 (38: 39) sts of front panel. 55 (55: 57) sts.
**Cont in patt, shaping sides by inc 1 st at each end of every foll 8th (8th: 6th) row (from previous inc) until there are 63 (83: 65) sts, taking inc sts into patt.

Small and large sizes only
Inc 1 st at each of every foll 10th (8th) row from previous inc until 79 (87) sts.
All sizes
Cont without further shaping until sleeve measures 43 cm, ending with a WS row.
Shape top
Keeping patt correct, cast off 4 (6: 8) sts at beg of next 2 rows. 71 sts.
Dec 1 st at each end of next 5 rows, then on foll 2 alt rows. 57 sts.
Work 3 rows, thus ending with a WS row.
Dec 1 st at each end of next and every foll 4th row until 43 sts rem.
Work 1 row, thus ending with a WS row.
Dec 1 st at each end of next and foll alt row. 39 sts.
Dec 1 st at each end of next 3 rows, thus ending with a WS row. 33 sts.
Cast off 4 sts at beg of next 4 rows.
Cast off rem 17 sts.

RIGHT SLEEVE
Back panel
Cast on 14 sts using 3mm (US 2/3) needles.
Row 1 (RS): *K1, P1, rep from * to end.
This row sets position of moss st as for back.
Work 25 rows more in moss st as now set, inc 1 st at end of 8th (8th: 6th) of these rows and every foll 8th (8th: 6th) row. 17 (17: 18) sts.
Break yarn and leave sts on a holder.
Front panel
Cast on 40 sts using 3mm (US 2/3) needles.
Row 1 (RS): *P1, K1, rep from * to end.
This row sets position of moss st as for back.
Work 25 rows more in moss st as now set, inc 1 st at beg of 8th (8th: 6th) of these rows and every foll 8th (8th: 6th) row. 43 (43: 44) sts.
Join panels
Row 27 (RS): Patt first 38 (38: 39) sts of front panel, with RS facing and holding front panel in front of back panel, patt tog next st of front panel with first st of back panel, (patt tog next st of each panel) 3 times, patt tog last st of front panel with next st of back panel, patt rem 12 (12: 13) sts of back panel. 55 (55: 57) sts.
Complete as for left sleeve from **.

V neck version
BACK and SLEEVES
Work as for high neck version.

LEFT FRONT
Work as for left front of high neck version to ***.
Cont without further shaping until 4 rows less have been worked than on back to start of armhole shaping, ending with a WS row.
Shape front slope
Next row (RS) (dec): Patt to last 10 sts, patt 3 tog, patt to end. 58 (62: 66) sts.
This row sets position of double dec worked 7 sts in from front opening edge.
Patt 3 rows, thus ending with a WS row.
Shape armhole
Keeping patt correct, cast off 4 (6: 8) sts at beg of next row. 54 (56: 58) sts.
Work 1 row.
Dec 1 st at armhole edge on next 7 rows, then on foll 4 alt rows **and at same time** dec 2 sts at front slope edge on every foll 8th row from previous dec, working front slope double dec 7 sts in from front opening edge as previously set. 39 (41: 43) sts.

33

Dec 2 sts at front slope edge **only** on every foll 8th row from previous dec, working front slope double dec 7 sts in from front opening edge as previously set, until 31 sts rem. Cont without further shaping until left front matches back to start of shoulder shaping, ending with a RS row.

Shape shoulder

Cast off 8 sts at beg of next and foll 2 alt rows.

Cont in patt on rem 7 sts for 6.5 (6.75: 7) cm for back neck extension. Cast off in patt. Mark positions for 7 buttons on this front - lowest button to be 9 rows above cast on edge, top button to be 4 rows below start of front slope shaping and rem 5 buttons evenly spaced between.

RIGHT FRONT

Work as for right front of high neck version to ****.

Complete to match left front of V neck version, reversing shapings.

MAKING UP

PRESS all pieces as described on the information page.

High neck version

Join both shoulder seams using back stitch.

Collar

Cast on 95 sts using 2³/₄mm (US 2) needles.

Row 1 (RS): K3, *P1, K1, rep from * to last 2 sts, K2.

This row sets position of moss st worked over centre sts with edge 3 sts worked as K sts on every row.

Keeping patt correct as now set, proceed as follows:

Work 1 row.

Next row (inc): K3, M1, patt to last 3 sts, M1, K3.

Work 2 rows, taking inc sts into moss st.

Rep last 3 rows until collar measures 8.5 cm. Cast off in patt.

Sew cast on edge of collar to neck edge, placing collar ends 4 sts in from front opening edge.

See info page for finishing instructions.

V neck version

Join both shoulder seams using back stitch.

Join cast off ends of back neck extensions, and then sew one edge to back neck.

See info page for finishing instructions.

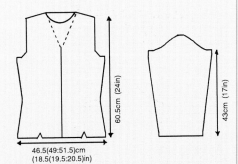

46.5(49:51.5)cm
(18.5(19.5:20.5)in)
60.5cm (24in)
43cm (17in)

Design number 7

Lola

KIM HARGREAVES

YARNS

Rowan Fine Cotton Chenille

	S	M	L	
Standard length				
(with collar & belt)	10	11	12	x 50gm
(Photographed in 418 Mousse)				
Longer length				
without collar or belt	10	11	12	x 50gm
collar & belt (optional)	3	3	3	x 50gm
(Photographed in 413 Black)				

NEEDLES

1 pair 2³/₄mm (no 12) (US 2) needles
1 pair 3¹/₄mm (no 10) (US 3) needles

BUTTONS -

5 for standard length
7 for longer length

TENSION

25 sts and 32 rows to 10 cm measured over patt using 3¹/₄mm (US 3) needles.

Pattern note: The pattern is written with the measurements given for the standard length first, followed by the longer length in **bold**.

SPECIAL ABBREVIATIONS

MB = Make bobble as folls: (K1, P1, K1, P1, K1) all into next st, turn, K5, turn, K5, lift 2nd, 3rd, 4th and 5th st over first st.

BACK

Cast on 122 (127: 132) sts using 3¹/₄mm (US 3) needles.

Row 1 (RS): K1, *K2tog, yfwd, K1, yfwd, sl 1, K1, psso, rep from * to last st, K1.

Row 2: Purl.

These 2 rows form patt.

Cont in patt until back measures 51 (**74**) cm, ending with a WS row.

Shape armholes

Keeping patt correct, cast off 6 sts at beg of next 2 rows. 110 (115: 120) sts.

Dec 1 st at each end of next 7 rows, then on foll 7 alt rows. 82 (87: 92) sts.

Cont without further shaping until armholes measure 20 cm, ending with a WS row.

Shape shoulders and back neck

Cast off 8 (8: 9) sts at beg of next 2 rows. 66 (71: 74) sts.

Next row (RS): Cast off 8 (8: 9) sts, patt until there are 11 (13: 13) sts on right needle and turn, leaving rem sts on a holder.

Work each side of neck separately.

Cast off 4 sts at beg of next row.

Cast off rem 7 (9: 9) sts.

With RS facing, rejoin yarn to rem sts, cast off centre 28 (29: 30) sts, patt to end.

Work to match first side, reversing shapings.

POCKET LININGS (make 2)

Cast on 32 sts using 3¹/₄mm (US 3) needles.

Starting with row 1, work in patt as for back until pocket lining measures 12.5 cm, ending with a WS row.

Break yarn and leave sts on a holder.

LEFT FRONT

Cast on 59 (62: 64) sts using 3¹/₄mm (US 3) needles.

Row 1 (RS): K1, *K2tog, yfwd, K1, yfwd, sl 1, K1, psso, rep from * to last 3 (1: 3) sts, [K2tog, yfwd] 1 (0: 1) times, K1.

Row 2: Purl.

These 2 rows form patt.

Cont in patt until left front measures 17.5 (**40.5**) cm, ending with a WS row.

Place pocket

Next row (RS): Patt 9 (12: 14), slip next 32 sts onto a holder and in their place patt across 32 sts of first pocket lining, patt 18.

Cont in patt until 8 rows less have been worked than on back to start of armhole shaping, thus ending with a WS row.

Shape front slope

Place marker at beg of last row to denote start of front slope shaping.

Dec 1 st at marked front slope edge on next and foll 4th row. 57 (60: 62) sts.

Work 3 rows, thus ending with a WS row.

Shape armhole

Keeping patt correct, cast off 6 sts at beg (armhole edge) and dec 1 st at end (front slope edge) of next row. 50 (53: 55) sts.

Work 1 row.

Dec 1 st at armhole edge on next 7 rows,

then on foll 7 alt rows **and at same time** dec 1 st at front slope edge on every foll 4th row from previous dec. 31 (34: 36) sts.
Now dec 1 st at front slope edge **only** on every foll 4th row from previous dec until 23 (25: 27) sts rem.
Cont without further shaping until left front matches back to start of shoulder shaping, ending with a **WS** row.

Shape shoulder
Cast off 8 (8: 9) sts at beg of next and foll alt row.
Work 1 row.
Cast off rem 7 (9: 9) sts.

RIGHT FRONT
Cast on 59 (62: 64) sts using 3¼mm (US 3) needles.
Row 1 (RS): K1, [yfwd, sl 1, K1, psso] 1 (0: 1) times, *K2tog, yfwd, K1, yfwd, sl 1, K1, psso, rep from * to last st, K1.
Row 2: Purl.
These 2 rows form patt.
Cont in patt until left front measures 17.5 (**40.5**) cm, ending with a WS row.

Place pocket
Next row (RS): Patt 18, slip next 32 sts onto a holder and in their place patt across 32 sts of second pocket lining, patt 9 (12: 14).
Complete to match left front, reversing shapings.

SLEEVES (both alike)
Cast on 52 sts using 3¼mm (US 3) needles.
Starting with row 1, cont in patt as for back, shaping sides by inc 1 st at each end of 7th and every foll 8th row until there are 84 sts, taking inc sts into patt.
Cont without further shaping until sleeve measures 43 cm, ending with a WS row.

Shape top
Keeping patt correct, cast off 6 sts at beg of next 2 rows. 72 sts.
Dec 1 st at each end of next 3 rows, then on foll 3 alt rows. 60 sts.
Work 3 rows, thus ending with a WS row.
Dec 1 st at each end of next and every foll 4th row until 52 sts rem.
Work 1 row, thus ending with a WS row.
Dec 1 st at each end of next and foll 4 alt rows. 42 sts.
Dec 1 st at each end of next 3 rows, thus ending with a WS row. 36 sts.
Cast off 4 sts at beg of next 4 rows.
Cast off rem 20 sts.

MAKING UP
PRESS all pieces as described on the information page.
Join both shoulder seams using back stitch.

Standard length version
Button border
With RS facing, using 2¾mm (US 2) needles, pick up and knit 106 sts evenly along left front opening edge between start of front slope shaping and cast on edge.
K 2 rows.
Cast off knitways.

Buttonhole border
With RS facing, using 2¾mm (US 2) needles, pick up and knit 106 sts evenly along right front opening edge between cast on edge and start of front slope shaping.
K 1 row.

Next row (RS) (buttonhole row):
K26, *(yfwd) twice (to make a st - drop extra loop on next row), K2tog, K17, rep from * 3 times more, (yfwd) twice (to make a st - drop extra loop on next row), K2tog, K2.
Cast off knitways.

Left collar
Cast on 3 sts using 2¾mm (US 2) needles.
Row 1 (RS): K3.
Row 2: Inc in first st, K2. 4 sts.
Row 3: K1, MB, K1, inc in last st. 5 sts.
Row 4: Inc in first st, K4. 6 sts.
Row 5: K2, (MB, K1) to end.
Row 6: Inc in first st, K to end. 7 sts.
Row 7: (K1, MB) to last st, inc in last st. 8 sts.
Row 8: Knit.
Row 9: K1, (K1, MB) to last st, inc in last st. 9 sts.
Row 10: Inc in first st, K to end. 10 sts.
Row 11: (K1, MB) to last 2 sts, K2.
Row 12: Inc in first st, K to end. 11 sts.
Row 13: K2, (MB, K1) to last st, inc in last st. 12 sts.
Row 14: Knit.
Row 15: (K1, MB) to last 2 sts, K1, inc in last st. 13 sts.
Row 16: Inc in first st, K to end. 14 sts.
Rows 17 to 28: As rows 5 to 16. 22 sts.
Row 29: K2, (MB, K1) to end.
Row 30: Inc in first st, K to end. 23 sts.
Row 31: (K1, MB) to last st, K1.
Row 32: Inc in first st, K to end. 24 sts.
Rows 33 to 40: As rows 29 to 32, twice. 28 sts.
Keeping patt correct as now set, work 3 rows, thus ending with a RS row.
Inc 1 st at beg of next and every foll 4th row until there are 33 sts, taking inc sts into patt.
Cont without further shaping until shaped edge fits up left front slope from top of button border and across to centre back neck.
Cast off.

Right collar
Cast on 3 sts using 2¾mm (US 2) needles.
Row 1 (RS): K3.
Row 2: K2, inc in last st. 4 sts.
Row 3: Inc in first st, K1, MB, K1. 5 sts.
Row 4: K3, inc in last st. 6 sts.
Row 5: (K1, MB) to last 2 sts, K2.
Row 6: K to last st, inc in last st. 7 sts.
Row 7: Inc in first st, (MB, K1) to end. 8 sts.
Row 8: Knit.
Row 9: Inc in first st, (MB, K1) to last st, K1. 9 sts.
Row 10: K to last st, inc in last st. 10 sts.
Row 11: K2, (MB, K1) to end.
Row 12: K to last st, inc in last st. 11 sts.
Row 13: Inc in first st, (K1, MB) to last 2 sts, K2. 12 sts.
Row 14: Knit.
Row 15: Inc in first st, K1, (MB, K1) to end. 13 sts.
Row 16: K to last st, inc in last st. 14 sts.
Rows 17 to 28: As rows 5 to 16. 22 sts.
Row 29: (K1, MB) to last 2 sts, K2.
Row 30: K to last st, inc in last st. 23 sts.
Row 31: (K1, MB) to last st, K1.
Row 32: K to last st, inc in last st. 24 sts.
Rows 33 to 40: As rows 29 to 32, twice. 28 sts.
Complete to match left collar, reversing shapings.

Join cast off edges of collar pieces. Sew collar to neck edge, matching cast on edges to top of button and buttonhole borders and collar seam to centre back neck.

Belt
Cast on 325 sts using 2¾mm (US 2) needles.
K 8 rows.
Cast off loosely and evenly knitways.

Longer length version
Button border
With RS facing, using 2¾mm (US 2) needles and starting at centre back neck, pick up and knit 18 (19: 19) sts from centre back neck to shoulder seam, 56 sts down left front slope to start of front slope shaping, and 134 sts evenly down left front opening edge to cast on edge. 208 (209: 209) sts.
K 2 rows.
Cast off knitways.

Buttonhole border
With RS facing, using 2¾mm (US 2) needles and starting at cast on edge, pick up and knit 134 sts evenly up right front opening edge to start of front slope shaping, 56 sts up right front slope to shoulder seam, and 18 (19: 19) sts across to centre back neck. 208 (209: 209) sts.
K 1 row.

Next row (RS) (buttonhole row):
K35, *(yfwd) twice (to make a st - drop extra loop on next row), K2tog, K14, rep from * 5 times more, (yfwd) twice (to make a st - drop extra loop on next row), K2tog, K to end.
Cast off knitways.

Both versions
Pocket tops
Slip 32 pocket sts onto 2¾mm (US 2) needles and rejoin yarn with RS facing.
K 4 rows.
Cast off knitways.
See information page for finishing instructions.

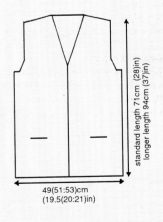

standard length 71cm (28)in
longer length 94cm (37)in

49(51:53)cm
(19.5(20:21)in)

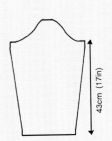

43cm (17in)

Design number 8

Royal

KIM HARGREAVES

YARNS

Rowan Chunky Chenille

One colour version

childrens

8-9	9-11	12-14	yrs
6	7	8	x 100gm

(Photographed in 356 Aubergine)

ladies

S	M	L	
8	9	9	x 100gm

(Not photographed)

Four colour version

ladies		S	M	L	
A Elephant	348	6	7	7	x100gm
B Blackcurrant	381	1	1	1	x100gm
C French Mustard	363	1	2	2	x100gm
D Fern	364	1	1	1	x100gm

NEEDLES

1 pair 3³/₄mm (no 9) (US 5) needles
1 pair 4¹/₂mm (no 7) (US 7) needles

TENSION

19 sts and 20 rows to 10 cm measured over patt using 4¹/₂mm (US 7) needles.

Pattern note: The pattern is written for the three childrens sizes, followed by the ladies sizes in **bold**.

Colour note: References to yarn A, B, C and D are for ladies sizes only. Childrens sizes are knitted in one colour throughout.

BACK

Cast on 93 (97: 101: **105: 111: 117**) sts using 3³/₄mm (US 5) needles and yarn A.
Beg with P row, work 4 rows in reverse st st.
Change to 4¹/₂mm (US 7) needles.

Childrens sizes only

Row 1 (RS): K1, K2tog, K5 (7: 9), M1, *K1, M1, K7, sl 1, K1, psso, K2tog, K7, M1, rep from * to last 9 (11: 13) sts, K1, M1, K5 (7: 9), sl 1, K1, psso, K1.
Row 2: Purl.
These 2 rows form patt.

Ladies sizes only

Row 1 (RS): K1, K2tog, K(**3: 6: 9**), yfwd, *K1, yfwd, K9, sl 1, K1, psso, K2tog, K9, yfwd, rep from * to last (**7: 10: 13**) sts, K1, yfwd, K(**3: 6: 9**), sl 1, K1, psso, K1.
Row 2: Purl.
These 2 rows form patt.
Joining in and breaking off colours as required, cont in patt as now set, working in foll stripe sequence throughout: a further 8 rows using yarn A, 8 rows using yarn B, 6 rows using yarn A, 10 rows using yarn C, 6 rows using yarn D, 10 rows using yarn C, 6 rows using yarn A, 8 rows using yarn B, and then cont using yarn A only.

All sizes

Cont straight until back measures 38 (40: 42: **48.5: 51: 53.5**) cm, end with a WS row.

Shape armholes

Keeping patt correct, cast off 4 sts at beg of next 2 rows. 85 (89: 93: **97: 103: 109**) sts.

Childrens sizes only

Dec 1 st at each end of next 4 rows. 77 (81: 85) sts.

Ladies sizes only

Dec 1 st at each end of next 5 rows, then on foll 5 alt rows. (**77: 83: 89**) sts.

All sizes

Cont without further shaping until armholes measures 20 (21: 22: **25: 25: 25**) cm, ending with a WS row.

Shape back neck and shoulders

Next row (RS): Patt until there are 29 (30: 31: **24: 27: 30**) sts on right needle and turn, leaving rem sts on a holder.
Work each side of neck separately.
Cast off 4 sts at beg of row.
Cast off rem 25 (26: 27: **20: 23: 26**) sts.
With RS facing, rejoin yarn to rem sts, cast off centre 19 (21: 23: **29: 29: 29**) sts, patt to end.
Work to match first side, reversing shapings.

FRONT

Work as for back until 14 (14: 14: **16: 16: 16**) rows less have been worked before start of shoulder shaping, ending with a WS row.

Shape neck

Next row (RS): Patt 32 (33: 34: **31: 34: 37**) and turn, leaving rem sts on a holder.
Work each side of neck separately.

Ladies sizes only

Cast off 4 sts at beg of next row. (**27: 30: 33**) sts.

All sizes

Dec 1 st at neck edge on next 4 (4: 4: **3: 3: 3**) rows, then on foll 3 (3: 3: **4: 4: 4**) alt rows. 25 (26: 27: **20: 23: 26**) sts.
Work 3 rows, thus ending with a WS row.

Shape shoulder

Cast off rem 25 (26: 27: **20: 23: 26**) sts.
With RS facing, rejoin yarn to rem sts, cast off centre 13 (15: 17: **15: 15: 15**) sts, patt to end.
Work to match first side, reversing shapings.

SLEEVES (both alike)

Cast on 43 (47: 51: **57: 57: 57**) sts using 3³/₄mm (US 5) needles and yarn A.
Beg with P row, work 4 rows in reverse st st.
Change to 4¹/₂mm (US 7) needles.

Childrens sizes only

Row 1 (RS): K3 (5: 7), *M1, K7, sl 1, K1, psso, K2tog, K7, M1, K1, rep from * once more, K2 (4: 6).
Row 2: Purl.
These 2 rows set position of patt as for back.

Ladies sizes only

Row 1 (RS): K1, K2tog, K2, yfwd, *K1, yfwd, K9, sl 1, K1, psso, K2tog, K9, yfwd, rep from * once more, K1, yfwd, K2, sl 1, K1, psso, K1.
Row 2: Purl.
These 2 rows set position of patt as for back.
Joining in and breaking off colours as required, cont in patt as now set, working in same stripe sequence as for back.

All sizes

Keeping patt correct, cont in patt, shaping sides by inc 1 st at each end of next and every foll 4th row to 67 (63: 65: **87: 87: 87**) sts, then on every foll 6th row (from previous inc) until there are 77 (79: 83: **95: 95: 95**) sts, taking inc sts into patt.
Cont without further shaping until sleeve measures 44 (45: 46: **49: 49: 49**) cm, ending with a WS row.

Shape top

Cast off 4 sts at beg of next 2 rows. 69 (71: 75: **87: 87: 87**) sts.

Ladies sizes only

Dec 1 st at each end of next and foll 4 alt rows. 77 sts.

All sizes

Dec 1 st at each end of next 4 (4: 4: **5: 5: 5**) rows. Cast off rem 61 (63: 67: **67: 67: 67**) sts loosely and evenly.

MAKING UP

Note: Due to the nature of the st pattern, cast off edges are NOT straight, but form wavy edges. When seaming pieces together, straighten wavy edge(s) by varying amount taken into seam.
Join right shoulder seam using back stitch.

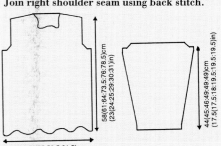

58(61:64:73.5:76:78.5)cm
(23(24:25:29:30:31)in)

44(45:46:49:49:49)cm
(17.5(17.5:18:19.5:19.5:19.5)in)

49(51:53:55:58.5:61.5)cm
(19.5(20:21:21.5:23:24)in)

36

Neckband

With RS facing and using 3³/₄mm (US 5) needles, pick up and knit 14 (14: 14: **18: 18: 18**) sts down left front neck, 13 (15: 17: **15: 15: 15**) sts across centre front, 14 (14: 14: **18: 18: 18**) sts up right front neck and 27 (29: 31: **37: 37: 37**) sts across back neck. 68 (72: 76: **88: 88: 88**) sts.
Starting with a K row, work 4 rows in reverse st st.
Cast off loosely and evenly knitways.
See information page for finishing instructions.

Design number 9

Sheba

KIM HARGREAVES

YARNS

Rowan Chunky Chenille

	S	M	L	
Buttoned version	6	6	7	x100gm
Zipped version	6	6	7	x100gm

(Buttoned version photographed in 379 Chocolate, zipped version in 356 Aubergine)

NEEDLES

1 pair 3³/₄mm (no 9) (US 5) needles
1 pair 4¹/₂mm (no 7) (US 7) needles

BUTTONS (buttoned version only) - 6

ZIP (zipped version only) - 61 cm (24 in) long open ended zip

TENSION

16 sts and 24 rows to 10 cm measured over st st using 4¹/₂mm (US 7) needles.

BACK

Buttoned version only
Cast on 72 (76: 80) sts using 3³/₄mm (US 5) needles.
Knit 10 rows, thus ending with a WS row.
Zipped version only
Cast on 74 (78: 82) sts using 3³/₄mm (US 5) needles.
Row 1 (RS): K2, *P2, K2, rep from * to end.
Row 2: P2, *K2, P2, rep from * to end.
Rep these 2 rows 4 times more, dec 1 st at each end of last row. 72 (76: 80) sts.
Both versions
Change to 4¹/₂ mm needles.
Beg with a K row, work 12 rows in st st, thus ending with a WS row.
Shape side seams and darts
Place markers on 18th (19th: 20th) sts from each end of last row.
Row 23 (RS) (dec): K2tog, (K to 2 sts before marked st, sl 1, K1, psso, K marked st, K2tog) twice, K to last 2 sts, K2tog. 66 (70: 74) sts.
Work 5 rows.
Rep last 6 rows twice more and then row 23 again. 48 (52: 56) sts.
Work 13 rows, thus ending with a WS row.
Row 55 (RS) (inc): Inc in first st, (K to marked st, M1, K marked st, M1) twice, K to last st, inc in last st. 54 (58: 62) sts.
Work 7 rows.
Rep last 8 rows twice more, and then row 55 again. 72 (76: 80) sts.
Cont straight until back measures 41 cm, ending with a WS row.
Shape armholes
Cast off 3 (4: 5) sts at beg of next 2 rows. 66 (68: 70) sts.
Dec 1 st at each end of next 3 rows, then on foll 5 alt rows. 50 (52: 54) sts.
Cont without further shaping until armholes measures 20 cm, ending with a WS row.
Shape shoulders and back neck
Cast off 5 sts at beg of next 2 rows. 40 (42: 44) sts.
Next row (RS): Cast off 5 sts, K until there are 8 (9: 10) sts on right needle and turn, leaving rem sts on a holder.
Work each side of neck separately.
Cast off 4 sts at beg of next row.
Cast off rem 4 (5: 6) sts.
With RS facing, rejoin yarn to rem sts, cast off centre 14 sts, K to end.
Work to match first side, reversing shapings.

LEFT FRONT

Buttoned version only
Cast on 40 (42: 44) sts using 3³/₄mm (US 5) needles.
Knit 9 rows, thus ending with a RS row.
Row 10 (WS): K6 and slip these 6 sts onto

a safety pin for button border, M1, K to end. 35 (37: 39) sts.
Change to 4¹/₂ mm needles.
Beg with a K row, work 12 rows in st st, thus ending with a WS row.
Zipped version only
Cast on 39 (39: 43) sts using 3³/₄mm (US 5) needles.
Row 1 (RS): *K2, P2, rep from * to last 3 sts, K3.
Row 2: K1, P2, *K2, P2, rep from * to end.
Rep these 2 rows 4 times more, dec 3 (1: 3) sts evenly on last row. 36 (38: 40) sts.
Change to 4¹/₂ mm needles.
Row 11 (RS): Knit.
Row 12: K1, P to end.
These 2 rows set position of st st with front opening edge st worked as a K st on every row. (**Note:** this edge st forms finished front opening edge and, as such, it is best to join in new balls of yarn at opposite end of rows, thereby leaving this edge smooth and neat.)
Work a further 10 rows, end with a WS row.
Both versions
Shape side seam and dart
Place marker on 18th (19th: 20th) st from end of last row.
(**Note:** Stitch counts given from this point are for buttoned version. Stitch counts for zipped version are one st greater than stated.)
Row 23 (RS) (dec): K2tog, K to 2 sts before marked st, sl 1, K1, psso, K marked st, K2tog, K to end. 32 (34: 36) sts.
Work 5 rows.
Rep last 6 rows twice more and then row 23 again. 23 (25: 27) sts.
Work 13 rows, thus ending with a WS row.
Row 55 (RS) (inc): Inc in first st, K to marked st, M1, K marked st, M1, K to end. 26 (28: 30) sts.
Work 7 rows.
Rep last 8 rows twice more, and then row 55 again. 35 (37: 39) sts.
Cont straight until left front matches back to start of armhole shaping, end with a WS row.
Shape armhole
Cast off 3 (4: 5) sts at beg of next row. 32 (33: 34) sts.
Work 1 row.
Dec 1 st at armhole edge on next 3 rows, then on foll 5 alt rows. 24 (25: 26) sts.
Cont without further shaping until 15 rows less have been worked than on back to start of shoulder shaping, ending with a RS row.
Shape neck
Buttoned version only
Cast off 4 sts at beg of next row. 20 (21: 22) sts.
Zipped version only
Cast off 5 sts at beg of next row. 20 (21: 22) sts.
Both versions
(**Note:** Stitch counts given are now same for both versions.)
Dec 1 st at neck edge on next 3 rows, then on foll 2 alt rows. 15 (16: 17) sts.
Work 3 rows.
Dec 1 st at neck edge on next row. 14 (15: 16) sts.
Work 3 rows, thus ending with a WS row.
Shape shoulder
Cast off 5 sts at beg of next and foll alt row.
Work 1 row.
Cast off rem 4 (5: 6) sts.

RIGHT FRONT

Buttoned version only

Cast on 40 (42: 44) sts using 3³/₄mm (US 5) needles.
Knit 9 rows, thus ending with a RS row.
Row 10 (WS): K to last 6 sts, M1 and turn, leaving last 6 sts on a safety pin for buttonhole border. 35 (37: 39) sts.
Change to 4¹/₂ mm needles.
Beg with a K row, work 12 rows in st st, thus ending with a WS row.

Zipped version only

Cast on 39 (39: 43) sts using 3³/₄mm (US 5) needles.
Row 1 (RS): K3, *P2, K2, rep from * to end.
Row 2: *P2, K2, rep from * to last 3 sts, P2, K1.
Rep these 2 rows 4 times more, dec 3 (1: 3) sts evenly on last row. 36 (38: 40) sts.
Change to 4¹/₂ mm needles.
Row 11 (RS): Knit.
Row 12: P to last st, K1.
These 2 rows set position of st st with front opening edge st worked as a K st on every row. (**Note:** this edge st forms finished front opening edge and, as such, it is best to join in new balls of yarn at opposite end of rows, thereby leaving this edge smooth and neat.)
Work a further 10 rows, end with a WS row.

Both versions

Shape side seam and dart

Place marker on 18th (19th: 20th) st from beg of last row.
(**Note:** Stitch counts given from this point are for buttoned version. Stitch counts for zipped version are one st greater than stated.)
Row 23 (RS) (dec): K to 2 sts before marked st, sl 1, K1, psso, K marked st, K2tog, K to last 2 sts, K2tog. 32 (34: 36) sts.
Work 5 rows.
Rep last 6 rows twice more and then row 23 again. 23 (25: 27) sts.
Work 13 rows, thus ending with a WS row.
Row 55 (RS) (inc): K to marked st, M1, K marked st, M1, K to last st, inc in last st. 26 (28: 30) sts.
Work 7 rows.
Rep last 8 rows twice more, and then row 55 again. 35 (37: 39) sts.
Complete to match left front, rev shapings.

SLEEVES

Cast on 34 sts using 3³/₄mm (US 5) needles.

Buttoned version only

Knit 10 rows, thus ending with a WS row.

Zipped version only

Work 20 rows in rib as given for back, thus ending with a WS row.

Both versions

Place markers at both ends of last row.
Change to 4¹/₂ mm needles.
Beg with a K row, work in st st, shaping sides by inc 1 st at each end of 3rd and every foll 8th (8th: 6th) row to 40 (50: 38) sts, then on every foll 10th (10th: 8th) row from previous inc until there are 52 (54: 56) sts.
Cont without further shaping until sleeve measures 40 cm from markers, ending with a WS row.

Shape top

Cast off 3 (4: 5) sts at beg of next 2 rows. 46 sts.
Dec 1 st at each end of next 3 rows, then on

foll alt row. 38 sts.
Work 3 rows, thus ending with a WS row.
Dec 1 st at each end of next and every foll 4th row until 28 sts rem.
Work 1 row, thus ending with a WS row.
Dec 1 st at each end of next 4 rows, thus ending with a WS row. 20 sts.
Cast off 4 sts at beg of next 2 rows.
Cast off rem 12 sts.

MAKING UP

PRESS all pieces as described on the information page.

Buttoned version

Join both shoulder seams using back stitch.

Button border

Slip 6 sts left on left front safety pin onto 3³/₄mm (US 5) needles, rejoin yarn and with RS facing, cont in garter st until border, when slightly stretched, fits up front opening edge to neck shaping. Cast off.
Slip st border in position.
Mark positions for 6 buttons on this band - lowest button 4 cm above cast on edge, top button 1 cm below neck and rem 4 buttons evenly spaced between.

Buttonhole border

Work to match button border, rejoining yarn with WS facing and with the addition of 6 buttonholes worked to correspond with positions marked for buttons as folls:
Buttonhole row (RS): K1, K2tog, (yrn) twice (to make buttonhole - drop extra loop on next row), K3.

Collar

Cast on 102 sts using 3³/₄mm (US 5) needles.
K 2 rows.
Row 3: K13, sl 1, K2tog, psso, K to last 16 sts, sl 1, K2tog, psso, K13. 98 sts.
Row 4: Knit.
Row 5: K12, sl 1, K2tog, psso, K to last 15 sts, sl 1, K2tog, psso, K13. 94 sts.
Row 6: Knit.
Row 7: K11, sl 1, K2tog, psso, K to last 14 sts, sl 1, K2tog, psso, K11. 90 sts.
Row 8: Knit.
Cont in this way, working 1 less st before and after each dec, until 46 sts rem.
Cast off loosely knitways.
Sew cast off edge of collar to neck edge, positioning ends of collar midway across top of front borders.
See info page for finishing instructions.

Zipped version

Join both shoulder seams using back stitch.
Stopping stitching approx 8-10 cm below start of front neck shaping, sew zip in place behind front opening edges - approx 10 cm of zip will extend above neck at upper edge.

Collar

With RS facing and using 3³/₄mm (US 5) needles, pick up and knit 25 sts up right front neck, 22 sts across back neck, and 25 sts down left front neck. 72 sts.
Row 1 (WS): K1, *P2, K2, rep from * to last 3 sts, P2, K1.
Row 2: K3, *P2, K2, rep from * to last st, K1.
Rep last 2 rows for 10 cm.
Check top of zip will fit behind collar and cast off loosely in rib. (Work a few more or less rows as necessary so collar is correct length for zip.)
Sew remaining section of zip in place.
See information page for finishing instructions.

Design number 10

Blossom

KIM HARGREAVES

YARNS

Rowan Fine Cotton Chenille

S	M	L	
7	8	8	x 50gm

(Photographed in 416 marsh)

NEEDLES

1 pair 2³/₄mm (no 12) (US 2) needles
1 pair 3¹/₄mm (no 10) (US 3) needles

BUTTONS

5

TENSION

25 sts and 36 rows to 10 cm measured over st st using 3¹/₄mm (US 3) needles.

BACK

Cast on 120 (126: 132) sts using 2³/₄mm (US 2) needles.
Beg with a K row, work 10 rows in garter st.
Change to 3¹/₄mm (US 3) needles and cont in st st until back measures 25.5 (28: 30) cm, ending with a WS row.

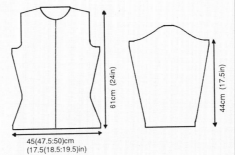

45(47.5:50)cm
(17.5(18.5:19.5)in)

61cm (24in)

44cm (17.5in)

Shape armholes

Cast off 4 sts at beg of next 2 rows.
112 (118: 124) sts.
Dec 1 st at each end of next 7 rows.
98 (104: 110) sts.
Work 1 row, thus ending with a WS row.
Dec 1 st at each end of next and foll 6 alt rows. 84 (90: 96) sts.
Cont without further shaping until armholes measure 20 cm, ending with a WS row.

Shape shoulders and back neck

Cast off 4 (5: 5) sts at beg of next 4 rows, then 5 (5: 6) sts at beg of foll 2 rows.
58 (60: 64) sts.

Next row (RS): Cast off 5 (5: 6) sts, K until there are 9 (10: 11) sts on right needle and turn, leaving rem sts on a holder.
Work each side of neck separately.
Cast off 4 sts at beg of next row.
Cast off rem 5 (6: 7) sts.
With RS facing, rejoin yarn to rem sts, cast off centre 30 sts, K to end.
Work to match first side, reversing shapings.

LEFT FRONT

Cast on 60 (63: 66) sts using 2³/₄mm (US 2) needles.
Beg with a K row, work 10 rows in garter st.
Change to 3¹/₄mm (US 3) needles and cont in st st until left front matches back to start of armhole shaping, ending with a WS row.

Shape armhole

Cast off 4 sts at beg of next row.
56 (59: 62) sts.
Work 1 row.
Dec 1 st at armhole edge on next 7 rows, then on foll 7 alt rows.
42 (45: 48) sts.
Cont without further shaping until 23 rows less have been worked than on back before start of shoulder shaping, thus ending with a RS row.

Shape neck

Cast off 5 sts at beg of next and foll alt row. 32 (35: 38) sts.
Dec 1 st at neck edge on next 3 rows, then on foll 4 alt rows. 25 (28: 31) sts.
Work 3 rows.
Dec 1 st at neck edge on next and foll 4th row. 23 (26: 29) sts.
Work 1 row, thus ending after a WS row.

Shape shoulder

Cast off 4 (5: 5) sts at beg of next and foll alt row, then 5 (5: 6) sts at beg of foll 2 alt rows.
Work 1 row.
Cast off rem 5 (6: 7) sts.

RIGHT FRONT

Work as for left front, reversing all shaping.

SLEEVES (both alike)

Cast on 50 sts using 2³/₄mm (US 2) needles.
Beg with a K row, work 10 rows in garter st.
Change to 3¹/₄mm (US 3) needles and cont in st st, shaping sides by inc 1 st at each end of 3rd and every foll 8th row to 72 sts, then on every foll 10th row (from previous inc) until there are 82 sts.
Cont without further shaping until sleeve measures 43 cm, ending with a WS row.

Shape top

Cast off 4 sts at beg of next 2 rows. 74 sts.
Dec 1 st at each end of next 5 rows, then on foll 3 alt rows. 58 sts.
Work 3 rows, thus ending with a WS row.

Dec 1 st at each end of next and every foll 4th row until 48 sts rem.
Work 1 row, thus ending with a WS row.
Dec 1 st at each end of next and foll 4 alt rows. 38 sts.
Dec 1 st at each end of next 3 rows, thus ending with a WS row. 32 sts.
Cast off 4 sts at beg of next 4 rows.
Cast off rem 16 sts loosely and evenly.

MAKING UP

PRESS all pieces as described on the information page.
Join both shoulder seams using back stitch.

Button border

With RS facing, using 2³/₄mm (US 2) needles, pick up and knit 102 sts evenly up left front opening edge.
Work 8 rows in garter st.
Cast off knitways.

Buttonhole border

With RS facing, using 2³/₄mm (US 2) needles, pick up and knit 102 sts evenly up right front opening edge.
Work 3 rows in garter st.
Row 4 (RS) (buttonhole row): K4, *cast off 2 sts, K until there are 21 sts on right needle after cast off, rep from * 3 times more, cast off 2 sts, K to end.
Row 5: K to end, casting on 2 sts over those cast off on previous row.
Work a further 3 rows in garter st.
Cast off knitways.

Collar

Cast on 148 sts using 2³/₄mm (US 2) needles.
K 2 rows.
Row 3: K15, sl 1, K2tog, psso, K to last 18 sts, sl 1, K2tog, psso, K15. 144 sts.
Row 4: Knit.
Row 5: K14, sl 1, K2tog, psso, K to last 17 sts, sl 1, K2tog, psso, K14. 140 sts.
Row 6: Knit.
Row 7: K13, sl 1, K2tog, psso, K to last 16 sts, sl 1, K2tog, psso, K13. 136 sts.
Row 8: Knit.
Cont in this way, working 1 less st before and after each dec, until 84 sts rem.
Cast off loosely knitways.
Sew cast off edge of collar to neck edge, positioning ends of collar midway across top of front borders.
See information page for finishing instructions.

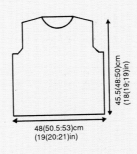

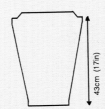

45.5(48:50)cm
(18(19:19)in)

48(50.5:53)cm
(19(20:21)in)

43cm
(17in)

India

KIM HARGREAVES

YARNS

Rowan Chunky Cotton Chenille

	S	M	L	
Shawl collared version	10	11	11	x100gm
High neck version	10	11	11	x100gm

(Shawl collared version photographed in 385 Tide, high neck version in 387 Navy)

NEEDLES

1 pair 3³/₄mm (no 9) (US 5) needles
1 pair 4mm (no 8) (US 6) needles
1 pair 4¹/₂mm (no 7) US 7) needles

BUTTONS - 6 for shawl collared version, or 7 for high neck version

TENSION

16 sts and 24 rows to 10 cm measured over moss st using 4¹/₂mm (US 7) needles.

BACK

Left back panel

Cast on 27 (28: 29) sts using 3³/₄mm (US 5) needles.

Row 1 (RS): Purl.
Row 2: Knit.
Rows 3 and 4: Purl.
Row 5: Knit.
Row 6: Purl.
These 6 rows form ridge patt.
Patt a further 9 rows.
Change to 4¹/₂ mm needles and patt another 3 rows, thus ending with a WS row.
Row 19 (RS): P5, K to end.
Row 20: P to last 5 sts, K5.
Last 2 rows set patt - edge 5 sts still worked in ridge patt with rem 22 (23: 24) sts now worked in st st.
Patt a further 16 rows, end with a WS row.
Break yarn and leave sts on a holder.
Centre back panel
Cast on 50 (52: 54) sts using 3³/₄mm (US 5) needles.
Work 15 rows in ridge patt as for left back panel.
Change to 4¹/₂ mm needles and patt another 3 rows, thus ending with a WS row.
Row 19 (RS): P5, K to last 5 sts, P5.
Row 20: K5, P to last 5 sts, K5.
Last 2 rows set patt - edge 5 sts still worked in ridge patt with centre 40 (42: 44) sts now worked in st st.
Patt a further 16 rows, end with a WS row.
Break yarn and leave sts on a holder.
Right back panel
Cast on 27 (28: 29) sts using 3³/₄mm (US 5) needles.
Work 15 rows in ridge patt as for left back panel.
Change to 4¹/₂ mm needles and patt another 3 rows, thus ending with a WS row.
Row 19 (RS): K to last 5 sts, P5.
Row 20: K5, P to end.
Last 2 rows set patt - edge 5 sts still worked in ridge patt with rem 22 (23: 24) sts now worked in st st.
Patt a further 16 rows, end with a WS row.
Join panels
Row 37 (RS): K first 22 (23: 24) sts of right back panel, with RS facing and holding centre back panel in front of right back panel, K tog next st of right back panel with first st of centre back panel, (K tog next st of each panel) 3 times, K tog last st of right back panel with next st of centre back panel, K next 40 (42: 44) sts of centre back panel, with RS facing and holding centre back panel in front of left back panel, K tog next st of centre back panel with first st of left back panel, (K tog next st of each panel) 3 times, K tog last st of centre back panel with next st of left back panel, K rem 22 (23: 24) sts of left back panel. 94 (98: 102) sts.
Beg with a P row, cont in st st until back measures 48 cm, ending with a WS row.
Shape armholes
Cast off 4 sts at beg of next 2 rows.
86 (90: 94) sts.
Dec 1 st at each end of next 8 rows.
70 (74: 78) sts.
Cont without further shaping until armholes measures 25.5 cm, ending with a WS row.
Shape shoulders and back neck
Cast off 7 (8: 8) sts at beg of next 2 rows.
56 (58: 62) sts.
Next row (RS): Cast off 7 (8: 8) sts, K until there are 11 (11: 13) sts on right needle and turn, leaving rem sts on a holder.
Work each side of neck separately.

Cast off 4 sts at beg of next row.
Cast off rem 7 (7: 9) sts.
With RS facing, rejoin yarn to rem sts, cast off centre 20 sts, K to end.
Work to match first side, reversing shapings.

POCKET LININGS (make 2)
Cast on 24 sts using 4¹/₂mm (US 7) needles.
Beg with a K row, work 30 rows in st st.
Break yarn and leave sts on a holder.

LEFT FRONT
Cast on 53 (55: 57) sts using 3³/₄mm (US 5) needles.
Work 14 rows in ridge patt as for left back panel.
Row 15 (RS): Patt to last 7 sts, M1 and turn, leaving last 7 sts on a safety pin for button border. 47 (49: 51) sts.
Change to 4¹/₂ mm needles.
Beg with a P row, work 29 rows in st st, thus ending with a WS row.
Place pocket
Next row (RS): K11 (12: 13), slip next 24 sts onto a holder and, in their place, K across 24 sts of first pocket lining, K12 (13: 14).
Cont in st st until left front matches back to start of armhole shaping, end with a WS row.
Shawl collared version only
Shape armhole and front slope
Place marker at beg of last row to denote start of front slope shaping.
Cast off 4 sts at beg and dec 1 st at end (marked front opening edge) of next row.
42 (44: 46) sts.
Work 1 row.
Dec 1 st at armhole edge on next 8 rows **and at same time** dec 1 st at front slope edge on every foll 4th row from previous dec.
32 (34: 36) sts.
Dec 1 st at front slope edge **only** on every foll 4th row from previous dec until 21 (23: 25) sts rem. Cont straight until left front matches back to start of shoulder shaping, end with a WS row.

High neck version only
Shape armhole
Cast off 4 sts at beg of next row.
43 (45: 47) sts.
Work 1 row.
Dec 1 st at armhole edge on next 8 rows.
35 (37: 39) sts.
Cont straight until 15 rows less have been worked than on back to start of shoulder shaping, ending with a RS row.
Shape neck
Cast off 5 sts at beg of next row and 4 sts at beg of foll alt row. 26 (28: 30) sts.
Dec 1 st at neck edge on next 3 rows, then on foll alt row. 22 (24: 26) sts.
Work 3 rows.
Dec 1 st at neck edge on next row.
21 (23: 25) sts.
Work 3 rows, thus ending with a WS row.
Both versions
Shape shoulder
Cast off 7 (8: 8) sts at beg of next and foll alt row.
Work 1 row. Cast off rem 7 (7: 9) sts.

RIGHT FRONT
Cast on 53 (55: 57) sts using 3³/₄mm (US 5) needles.

Work 14 rows in ridge patt as for left back panel.
Row 15 (RS): Patt 7 and slip these 7 sts onto a safety pin for buttonhole border, M1, patt to end. 47 (49: 51) sts.
Change to 4¹/₂ mm needles, beg with a P row, work 29 rows in st st, end with a WS row.
Place pocket
Next row (RS): K12 (13: 14), slip next 24 sts onto a holder and, in their place, K across 24 sts of second pocket lining, K11 (12: 13).
Complete to match left front, rev shapings.

SLEEVES
Cast on 56 sts using 4mm (US 6) needles.
Work 48 rows in ridge patt as for left back panel, thus ending with a cuff WS row.
(**Note:** WS of cuff now becomes RS of sleeve.)
Change to 4¹/₂mm (US 7) needles and beg with P row, cont in st st, shaping sides by inc 1 st at each end of 2nd and every foll 6th row to 68 sts, then on every foll 8th row until there are 80 sts.
Cont without further shaping until sleeve measures 56.5 cm, ending with a WS row.
Shape top
Cast off 4 sts at beg of next 2 rows. 72 sts.
Dec 1 st at each end of next 8 rows.
Cast off rem 56 sts.

MAKING UP
PRESS all pieces as described on the information page.
Join both shoulder seams using back stitch.
Shawl collared version
Button border and left collar
Slip 7 sts left on safety pin onto 3³/₄mm (US 5) needles and rejoin yarn with RS facing.
Cont in ridge patt as set until button border section, when slightly stretched, fits up front opening edge to start of front slope shaping, sewing in place as you go along and ending at inner edge (this is edge where border is attached to front).
Place marker at end of last row.
Keeping patt correct, inc 1 st at marked edge of next 2 rows. Work 1 row.
Rep last 3 rows 11 times more. 31 sts.
Cont in patt until collar, unstretched, fits up left front slope and across to centre back neck, ending at inner edge.
Cast off 8 sts at beg of next & foll 2 alt rows.
Work 1 row. Cast off rem 7 sts.
Mark positions for 6 buttons on button border section - first to be level with pocket opening, last to be 1.5 cm below start of front slope shaping and rem 4 evenly spaced between.
Buttonhole border and right collar
Slip 7 sts left on safety pin onto 3³/₄mm (US 5) needles and rejoin yarn with WS facing.
Complete to match button border and left collar with the addition of 6 buttonholes worked to match positions marked for buttons as folls:
Buttonhole row (RS): Patt 2, cast off 2, patt to end and back, casting on 2 sts over those cast off.
High neck version
Button border
Slip 7 sts left on safety pin onto 3³/₄mm (US 5) needles and rejoin yarn with RS facing.

40

Cont in ridge patt as set until button border, when slightly stretched, fits up front opening edge to neck shaping, sewing in place as you go along. Cast off.

Mark positions for 7 buttons on button border - the first level with pocket opening, last to be 1.5 cm below start of neck shaping and rem 5 evenly spaced between.

Buttonhole border

Slip 7 sts left on safety pin onto 3¾mm (US 5) needles and rejoin yarn with WS facing. Complete to match button border with the addition of 7 buttonholes worked to match positions marked for buttons as folls:

Buttonhole row (RS): Patt 2, cast off 2, patt to end and back, casting on 2 sts over those cast off.

Collar

Cast on 90 sts using 3¾mm (US 5) needles. Beg with a P row, work 3 rows in rev st st. Beg with a P row, work 3 rows in st st. Now work in patt as folls:

Row 1 (RS): P3, K to last 3 sts, P3.
Row 2: K3, P to last 3 sts, K3.
Row 3: As row 1.
Row 4: Purl.
Row 5: Knit.
Row 6: Purl.
Rep last 6 rows 3 times more, and then first 2 rows again.
Cast off loosely and evenly.
Sew cast off edge of collar to neck edge, placing ends of collar midway across top of front borders.

Both versions

Pocket tops

Slip 24 sts left on pocket holder onto 3¾mm (US 5) needles and rejoin yarn with RS facing.
Knit 3 rows. Cast off knitways (on WS).

Pocket flaps

Cast on 28 sts using 3¾mm (US 5) needles. Beg with a P row, work 3 rows in rev st st. Beg with a P row, work 3 rows in st st. Now work in patt as folls:

Row 1 (RS): P3, K to last 3 sts, P3.
Row 2: K3, P to last 3 sts, K3.
Row 3: As row 1.
Row 4: Purl.
Row 5: Knit.
Row 6: Purl.
Rep last 6 rows once more, and then first 5 rows again.
Cast off loosely and evenly.
Attach cast off edge of pocket flaps to fronts directly above pocket openings.
See info page for finishing instructions.

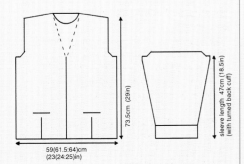

59(61.5:64)cm
(23(24:25)in)

73.5cm (29in)

sleeve length 47cm (18.5in) (with turned back cuff)

Design number 12

Musk

KIM HARGREAVES

YARNS

Rowan Chunky Cotton Chenille

	ladies			mens	
S	M	L	M	L	XL
11	11	12	12	13	13 x100gm

(Ladies photographed in 386 Lavender, mens in 378 Serge)

NEEDLES

1 pair 3¾mm (no 9) (US 5) needles
1 pair 4½mm (no 7) (US 7) needles
Cable needle

TENSION

16 sts and 24 rows to 10 cm measured over st st using 4½mm (US 7) needles.

Pattern note: The pattern is written for ladies sizes, followed by mens sizes in **bold**.

SPECIAL ABBREVIATIONS

C6F = Cable 6 front Slip next 3 sts onto cable needle and hold at front, K3, then K3 from cable needle.

C6B = Cable 6 back Slip next 3 sts onto cable needle and hold at back, K3, then K3 from cable needle.

BACK

Cast on 74 (78: 82: **86: 90: 94**) sts using 3¾mm (US 5) needles.

Row 1 (RS): K0 (0: 0: **0: 1: 0**), P0 (2: 0: **1: 2: 1**), [K2, P2] 4 (4: 5: **2: 2: 3**) times, *K3, P2, [K2, P2] twice, rep from * 3 (3: 3: **4: 4: 4**) times more, [K3, P2] 0 (0: 0: **1: 1: 1**) times, [K2, P2] 1 (2: **1: 2: 2**) times, K2 (0: 2: **2: 1: 2**), P0 (0: 0: **1: 0: 1**).

Row 2: P0 (0: 0: **0: 1: 0**), K0 (2: 0: **1: 2: 1**), [P2, K2] 4 (4: 5: **2: 2: 3**) times, *P3, K2, [P2, K2] twice, rep from * 3 (3: 3: **4: 4: 4**) times more, [P3, K2] 0 (0: 0: **1: 1: 1**) times, [P2, K2] 1 (2: **1: 2: 2**) times, P2 (0: 2: **2: 1: 2**), K0 (0: 0: **1: 0: 1**).

Rep these 2 rows 10 times more, and then row 1 again.
Change to 4½mm (US 7) needles.

Ladies sizes only

Row 24 (WS) (inc): P2 (0: 2), [K2, P2] 1 (2: 2) times, K2, [inc once in each of next 6 sts, K2, inc once in each of next 3 sts, K2] 4 times, inc once in each of next 6 sts, [K2, P2] 2 (2: 3) times, K0 (2: 0).
116 (120: 124) sts.

Mens sizes only

Row 24 (WS) (inc): K(**1: 0: 1**), P(**2: 1: 2**), [K2, P2] (**1: 2: 2**) times, K2, [inc once in each of next 3 sts, K2, inc once in each of next 6 sts, K2] 5 times, inc once in each of next 3 sts, [K2, P2] (**2: 2: 3**) times, K(**1: 2: 1**), P(**0: 1: 0**).
(**134: 138: 142**) sts.

All sizes

Cont in cable patt as folls:
Row 1 (RS): P8 (10: 12: **9: 11: 13**), [C6B, P2] 0 (0: 0: **1: 1: 1**) times, [C6B, C6F, P2, C6B, P2] twice, C6B, C6F, [P2, C6F, P2, C6B, C6F] twice, [P2, C6F] 0 (0: 0: **1: 1: 1**) times, P8 (10: 12: **9: 11: 13**).

Row 2 and every foll alt row: K8 (10: 12: **9: 11: 13**), [P6, K2] 0 (0: 0: **1: 1: 1**) times, [P12, K2, P6, K2] twice, P12, [K2, P6, K2, P12] twice, [K2, P6] 0 (0: 0: **1: 1: 1**) times, K8 (10: 12: **9: 11: 13**).

Row 3: P8 (10: 12: **9: 11: 13**), [K6, P2] 0 (0: 0: **1: 1: 1**) times, [K12, P2, K6, P2] twice, K12, [P2, K6, P2, K12] twice, [P2, K6] 0 (0: 0: **1: 1: 1**) times, P8 (10: 12: **9: 11: 13**).

Row 5: As row 3.
Row 7: As row 3.
Row 8: As row 2.
These 8 rows form cable patt.
Cont in patt until back measures 46 cm, ending with a WS row.

Shape armholes

Keeping patt correct, cast off 4 sts at beg of next 2 rows.
108 (112: 116: **126: 130: 134**) sts.
Dec 1 st at each end of next 3 (4: 4: **4: 4: 4**) rows.
102 (104: 108: **118: 122: 126**) sts.
Cont without further shaping until armholes measure 25.5 cm, ending with a WS row.

Shape shoulders and back neck

Keeping patt correct, cast off 10 (11: 11: **13: 14: 14**) sts at beg of next 2 rows.
82 (82: 86: **92: 94: 98**) sts.
(**Note:** To keep cast off edge from stretching, we recommend working [K2tog] 3

or 6 times across top of cables when casting off. St counts given refer to actual numbers of sts and do **NOT** take these decreases into account.)
Next row (RS): Cast off 10 (11: 11: **13: 14: 14**) sts, patt until there are 15 (14: 16: **17: 17: 19**) sts on right needle and turn, leaving rem sts on a holder.
Work each side of neck separately.
Cast off 4 sts at beg of next row.
Cast off rem 11 (10: 12: **13: 13: 15**) sts.
With RS facing, rejoin yarn to rem sts, cast off centre 32 sts, patt to end.
Work to match first side, reversing shapings.

FRONT
Work as for back until 18 rows less have been worked before start of shoulder shaping, thus ending with a WS row.
Shape neck
Next row (RS): patt 43 (44: 46: **51: 53: 55**) and turn, leave rem sts on a holder.
Work each side of neck separately.
Cast off 3 sts at beg of next and foll alt row.
37 (38: 40: **45: 47: 49**) sts.
Dec 1 st at neck edge on next 3 rows, then on foll 3 alt rows.
31 (32: 34: **39: 41: 43**) sts.
Work 5 rows, thus ending after a WS row.
Shape shoulder
Cast off 10 (11: 11: **13: 14: 14**) sts at beg of next and foll alt row.
Work 1 row.
Cast off rem 11 (10: 12: **13: 13: 15**) sts.
With RS facing, rejoin yarn to rem sts, cast off centre 16 sts, patt to end.
Work to match first side, reversing shapings.

SLEEVES (both alike)
Cast on 46 (46: 46: **50: 50: 50**) sts using 3³/₄mm (US 5) needles.
Row 1 (RS): K0 (0: 0: **2: 2: 2**), P2, *K3, P2, [K2, P2] twice, rep from * twice more, K3, P2, K0 (0: 0: **2: 2: 2**).
Row 2: P0 (0: 0: **2: 2: 2**), K2, *P3, K2, [P2, K2] twice, rep from * twice more, P3, K2, P0 (0: 0: **2: 2: 2**).
Rep these 2 rows 16 times more, and then row 1 again.
Change to 4¹/₂mm (US 7) needles.
Row 36 (WS) (inc): Inc in first st, P0 (0: 0: **1: 1: 1**), K1 (1: 1: **2: 2: 2**), *inc once in each of next 3 sts, K2, inc once in each of next 6 sts, K2, rep from * twice more, inc once in each of next 3 sts, K1 (1: 1: **2: 2: 2**), P0 (0: 0: **1: 1: 1**), inc in last st.
78 (78: 78: **82: 82: 82**) sts.
Cont in cable patt as folls:
Row 1 (RS): K1 (1: 1: **3: 3: 3**), P2, [K6, P2, K12, P2] 3 times, K6, P2, K1 (1: 1: **3: 3: 3**).
Row 2: P1 (1: 1: **3: 3: 3**), K2, [P6, K2, P12, K2] 3 times, P6, K2, P1 (1: 1: **3: 3: 3**).
Row 3: As row 1.
Row 4: As row 2.
Row 5: Inc in first st, K0 (0: 0: **2: 2: 2**), P2, [C6B, P2, C6B, C6F, P2] twice, C6F, P2, C6B, C6F, P2, C6F, P2, K0 (0: 0: **2: 2: 2**), inc in last st.
80 (80: 80: **84: 84: 84**) sts.
Row 6: P2 (2: 2: **4: 4: 4**), K2, [P6, K2, P12, K2] 3 times, P6, K2, P2 (2: 2: **4: 4: 4**).
Row 7: K2 (2: 2: **4: 4: 4**), P2, [K6, P2, K12, P2] 3 times, K6, P2, K2 (2: 2: **4: 4: 4**).

Row 8: As row 6.
These 8 rows set cable patt as for back.
Cont in patt, shaping sides by inc 1 st at each end of next and every foll 6th (6th: 6th: **8th: 8th: 8th**) row to 100 (100: 100: **98: 98: 98**) sts, then on every foll 8th (8th: 8th: **10th: 10th: 10th**) row until there are 104 sts, taking inc sts into patt.
Cont without further shaping until sleeve measures 53 (53: 53: **58: 58: 58**) cm, ending with a WS row.
Shape top
Cast off 4 sts at beg of next 2 rows. 96 sts.
Dec 1 st at each end of next 4 rows.
Cast off rem 88 sts, dec over cables as before.

MAKING UP
PRESS all pieces as described on the information page.
Join right shoulder seam using back stitch.
Neck border
With RS facing and using 3³/₄mm (US 5) needles, pick up and knit 19 sts down left front neck, 14 sts across centre front, 19 sts up right front neck and 30 sts across back neck. 82 sts.
Row 1: K2, *P2, K2, rep from * to end.
Row 2: P2, *K2, P2, rep from * to end.
Rep the last 2 rows for 12 (12: 12: **20: 20: 20**) cm.
Cast off loosely and evenly in rib.
See information page for finishing instructions.

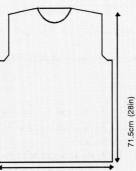

56.5(58.5:60.5:65.5:67.5:69.5)cm
(22(23:24:26:26.5:27.5)in)

71.5cm (28in)

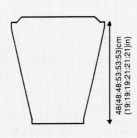

48(48:48:53:53:53)cm
(19:19:19:21:21:21)in)

Design number 13

Jet sweater and cardigan

KIM HARGREAVES

YARNS
Rowan Fine Cotton Chenille

	S	M	L		
Sweater	7	7	7	x	50gm

(Photographed in 418 Mousse)

| Cardigan | 7 | 7 | 7 | x | 50gm |

(Photographed in 407 Ruby)

NEEDLES
1 pair 2³/₄mm (no 12) (US 2) needles
1 pair 3¹/₄mm (no 10) (US 3) needles

BUTTONS (cardigan only)
9

TENSION
28 sts and 30 rows to 10 cm measured over patt using 3¹/₄mm (US 3) needles.

SWEATER and CARDIGAN BACK
Cast on 116 (122: 130) sts using 2³/₄mm (US 2) needles.

Beg with a P row, work 6 rows in reverse st st, thus ending with a WS row.
Change to 3¼mm (US 3) needles and cont in patt as folls:
Row 1 (RS): K6 (3: 1), [K2tog, K3, M1, K1] 0 (0: 1) times, [M1, K4, K2tog tbl] 0 (1: 1) times, *K2tog, K4, M1, K1, M1, K4, K2tog tbl, rep from * to last 6 (9: 13) sts, [K2tog, K4, M1] 0 (1: 1) times, [K1, M1, K3, K2tog tbl] 0 (0: 1) times, K6 (3: 1).
Row 2: Purl.
These 2 rows form patt.
Keeping patt correct and taking inc sts into patt, cont in patt, shaping side seams by inc 1 st at each end of next and every foll 10th row until there are 128 (134: 142) sts.
Cont without further shaping until back measures 25.5 (28: 30.5) cm, ending with a WS row.
Shape armholes
Keeping patt correct, cast off 6 sts at beg of next 2 rows.
116 (122: 130) sts.
Dec 1 st at each end of next 10 rows, then on every foll alt row until 84 (90: 98) sts rem.
Cont without further shaping until armholes measure 20 cm, ending with a WS row.
Shape shoulders and back neck
Cast off 7 (8: 9) sts at beg of next 2 rows.
70 (74: 80) sts.
Next row (RS): Cast off 7 (8: 9) sts, patt until there are 11 (12: 14) sts on right needle and turn, leaving rem sts on a holder.
Work each side of neck separately.
Cast off 4 sts at beg of next row.
Cast off rem 7 (8: 10) sts.
With RS facing, rejoin yarn to rem sts, cast off centre 34 sts, patt to end.
Work to match first side, reversing shapings.

SWEATER FRONT
Work as for back until 26 rows less have been worked before start of shoulder shaping, thus ending with a WS row.
Shape neck
Next row (RS): Patt 34 (37: 41) and turn, leave rem sts on a holder.
Work each side of neck separately.
Keeping patt correct, cast off 4 sts at beg of next row.
30 (33: 37) sts.
Dec 1 st at neck edge on next 3 rows, then on foll 4 alt rows.
23 (26: 30) sts.
Work 3 rows.
Dec 1 st at neck edge on next and foll 4th row. 21 (24: 28) sts.
Work 5 rows, thus ending with a WS row.
Shape shoulder
Cast off 7 (8: 9) sts at beg of next and foll alt row.
Work 1 row.
Cast off rem 7 (8: 10) sts.
With RS facing, rejoin yarn to rem sts, cast off centre 16 sts, patt to end.
Work to match first side, reversing shapings.

CARDIGAN POCKET LININGS (make 2)
Cast on 31 sts using 3¼mm (US 3) needles.
Row 1 (RS): K3, [M1, K4, K2tog tbl, K2tog, K4, M1, K1] twice, K2.
Row 2: Purl.
These 2 rows form patt.
Work a further 18 rows in patt.
Break yarn and leave sts on a holder.

CARDIGAN LEFT FRONT
Cast on 59 (62: 66) sts using 2¾mm (US 2) needles.
Beg with a P row, work 6 rows in reverse st st, thus ending with a WS row.
Change to 3¼mm (US 3) needles and cont in patt as folls:
Row 1 (RS): K6 (3: 1), [K2tog, K3, M1, K1] 0 (0: 1) times, [M1, K4, K2tog tbl] 0 (1: 1) times, *K2tog, K4, M1, K1, M1, K4, K2tog tbl, rep from * to last st, K1.
Row 2: Purl.
These 2 rows form patt.
Keeping patt correct and taking inc sts into patt, cont in patt, shaping side seam by inc 1 st at beg of next and foll 10th row.
61 (64: 68) sts.
Work 7 rows, thus ending with a WS row.
Place pocket
Next row (RS): Patt 12 (15: 19), slip next 31 sts onto a holder and in their place, patt across 31 sts of first pocket lining, patt 18.
Work 1 row.
Cont to shape side seam by inc 1 st at beg of next and every foll 10th row until there are 65 (68: 72) sts.
Cont without further shaping until left front matches back to start of armhole shaping, ending with a WS row.
Shape armholes
Keeping patt correct, cast off 6 sts at beg of next row.
59 (62: 66) sts.
Work 1 row.
Dec 1 st at armhole edge on next 10 rows, then on every foll alt row until 43 (46: 50) sts rem.
Cont without further shaping until 23 rows less have been worked than on back to start of shoulder shaping, ending with a RS row.
Shape neck
Keeping patt correct, cast off 8 sts at beg of next row, then 4 sts at beg of foll 2 alt rows.
27 (30: 34) sts.
Dec 1 st at neck edge on next 3 rows.
24 (27: 31) sts.
Work 1 row.
Dec 1 st at neck edge on next and every foll 4th row until 21 (24: 28) sts rem.
Work 5 rows, thus ending with a WS row.
Shape shoulder
Cast off 7 (8: 9) sts at beg of next and foll alt row.
Work 1 row.
Cast off rem 7 (8: 10) sts.

CARDIGAN RIGHT FRONT
Cast on 59 (62: 66) sts using 2¾mm (US 2) needles.
Beg with a P row, work 6 rows in reverse st st, thus ending with a WS row.
Change to 3¼mm (US 3) needles and cont in patt as folls:
Row 1 (RS): K1, *K2tog, K4, M1, K1, M1, K4, K2tog tbl, rep from * to last 6 (9: 13) sts, [K2tog, K4, M1] 0 (1: 1) times, [K1, M1, K3, K2tog tbl] 0 (0: 1) times, K6 (3: 1).
Row 2: Purl.
These 2 rows form patt.
Keeping patt correct and taking inc sts into patt, cont in patt, shaping side seam by inc 1 st at end of next and foll 10th row.
61 (64: 68) sts.
Work 7 rows, thus ending with a WS row.

Place pocket
Next row (RS): Patt 18, slip next 31 sts onto a holder and in their place, patt across 31 sts of second pocket lining, patt 12 (15: 19).
Complete to match left front, reversing shapings.

SWEATER AND CARDIGAN SLEEVES
Cast on 56 sts using 2¾mm (US 2) needles.
Beg with a P row, work 6 rows in reverse st st, thus ending with a WS row.
Change to 3¼mm (US 3) needles and cont in patt as folls:
Row 1 (RS): K2, *K2tog, K4, M1, K1, M1, K4, K2tog tbl, rep from * to last 2 sts, K2.
Row 2: Purl.
These 2 rows form patt.
Keeping patt correct and taking inc sts into patt, cont in patt, shaping sides by inc 1 st at each end of next and every foll 6th row to 86 sts, then on every foll 8th row until there are 92 sts.
Cont without further shaping until sleeve measures 43 cm, ending with a WS row.
Shape top
Keeping patt correct, cast off 6 sts at beg of next 2 rows.
80 sts.
Dec 1 st at each end of next 3 rows, then on every foll alt row until 68 sts rem.
Work 3 rows.
Dec 1 st at each end of next and every foll 4th row until 62 sts rem, then on every foll alt row until 52 sts rem.
Dec 1 st at each end of next 3 rows, thus ending with a WS row.
46 sts.
Cast off 4 sts at beg of next 6 rows.
Cast off rem 22 sts.

MAKING UP
PRESS all pieces as described on the information page.

Sweater only
Join right shoulder seam using back stitch.
Neck border
With RS facing and using 2¾mm (US 2) needles, pick up and knit 30 sts down left front neck, 16 sts across centre front, 30 sts up right front neck and 40 sts across back neck.
116 sts.
Beg with a K row, work 6 rows in rev st st.
Cast off loosely and evenly knitways.
See information page for finishing instructions.

Cardigan only
Join both shoulder seams using back stitch.
Button border
With RS facing and using 2¾mm (US 2) needles, pick up and knit 94 (102: 110) sts down left front opening edge.
Beg with a K row, work 6 rows in rev st st.
Cast off knitways.
Buttonhole border
Work as for button border, picking up sts up right front opening edge and with the addition of 9 buttonholes in 3rd row as folls:
Buttonhole row (WS): K2, [K2tog, (yrn) twice (to make a buttonhole - drop extra loop on next row), K9 (10: 11)] 8

times, K2tog, (yrn) twice (to make a buttonhole - drop extra loop on next row), K2.

Neck border

With RS facing and using 2³/₄mm (US 2) needles, pick up and knit 1 st from inside edge of buttonhole border, 38 sts up right front neck to shoulder, 40 sts across back neck, 38 sts down left front neck, and 1 st from inside edge of button border. 118 sts.

Beg with a K row, work 6 rows in rev st st. Cast off knitways.

Pocket tops

Slip 31 sts left on pocket holder onto 2³/₄mm (US 2) needles and rejoin yarn with RS facing.

Beg with a P row, work 5 rows in rev st st. Cast off knitways.

See information page for finishing instructions.

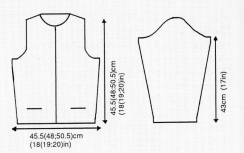

45.5(48;50.5)cm (18(19;20)in)

45.5(48:50.5)cm (18(19.20)in)

43cm (17in)

Design number 14

George sweater

KIM HARGREAVES

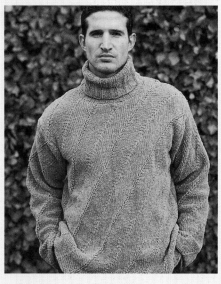

YARNS

Rowan Chunky Chenille

	ladies			mens	
S	M	L	M	L	XL

Polo neck version

| 8 | 9 | 9 | 9 | 10 | 10 x100gm |

Hooded version

| 9 | 9 | 10 | - | - | - x100gm |

(Ladies photographed in 385 Tide, mens in 383 Parchment)

NEEDLES

1 pair 4¹/₂mm (no 7) (US 7) needles

TENSION

16 sts and 28 rows to 10 cm measured over patt using 4¹/₂mm (US 7) needles.

Pattern note: The pattern is written for the ladies sizes, followed by the mens sizes in **bold**.

BACK

Cast on 93 (97: 101: **101: 105: 109**) sts using 4¹/₂mm (US 7) needles.

Row 1 (RS): K0 (1: 1: **1: 3: 5**), [K2tog tbl, inc purlways in next st] 0 (0: 1: **1: 1: 1**) times, P9 (10: 9: **9: 9: 9**), *P2tog, inc knitways in next st, K9, K2tog tbl, inc purlways in next st, P9, rep from * to last 12 (14: 16: **16: 18: 20**) sts, P2tog, inc knitways in next st, K9 (11: 9: **9: 9: 9**), [K2tog tbl, inc purlways in next st] 0 (0: 1: **1: 1: 1**) times, P0 (0: 1: **1: 3: 5**).

Row 2: K0 (1: 3: **3: 5: 7**), P11 (12: 12: **12: 12: 12**), *K12, P12, rep from * to last 10 (12: 14: **14: 16: 18**) sts, K10 (12: 12: **12: 12: 12**), P0 (0: 2: **2: 4: 6**).

Row 3: K0 (0: 0: **0: 2: 4**), [K2tog tbl, inc purlways in next st] 0 (0: 1: **1: 1: 1**) times, P8 (9: 9: **9: 9: 9**), *P2tog, inc knitways in next st, K9, K2tog tbl, inc purlways in next st, P9, rep from * to last 13 (16: 17: **17: 19: 21**) sts, P2tog, inc knitways in next st, K10 (10: 9: **9: 9: 9**), [K2tog tbl, inc purlways in next st] 0 (1: 1: **1: 1: 1**) times, P0 (0: 2: **2: 4: 6**).

Row 4: K0 (2: 4: **4: 6: 8**), P12, *K12, P12, rep from * to last 9 (11: 13: **13: 15: 17**) sts, K9 (11: 12: **12: 12: 12**), P0 (0: 1: **1: 3: 5**).

Row 5: K0 (0: 1: **1: 1: 3**), [K2tog tbl, inc purlways in next st] 0 (0: 0: **0: 1: 1**) times, P7 (9: 10: **10: 9: 9**), *P2tog, inc knitways in next st, K9, K2tog tbl, inc purlways in next st, P9, rep from * to last 14 (16: 18: **18: 20: 22**) sts, P2tog, inc knitways in next st, K11 (9: 9: **9: 9: 9**), [K2tog tbl, inc purlways in next st] 0 (1: 1: **1: 1: 1**) times, P0 (1: 3: **3: 5: 7**).

Row 6: K1 (3: 5: **5: 7: 9**), P12, *K12, P12, rep from * to last 8 (10: 12: **12: 14: 16**) sts, K8 (10: 12: **12: 12: 12**), P0 (0: 0: **0: 2: 4**).

Row 7: K0 (0: 0: **0: 0: 2**), [K2tog tbl, inc purlways in next st] 0 (0: 0: **0: 1: 1**) times, P6 (8: 10: **10: 9: 9**), *P2tog, inc knitways in next st, K9, K2tog tbl, inc purlways in next st, P9, rep from * to last 15 (17: 19: **19: 21: 23**) sts, P2tog, inc knitways in next st, K9, K2tog tbl, inc purlways in next st, P0 (2: 4: **4: 6: 8**).

Row 8: K2 (4: 6: **6: 8: 10**), P12, *K12, P12, rep from * to last 7 (9: 11: **11: 13: 15**) sts, K7 (9: 11: **11: 12: 12**), P0 (0: 0: **0: 1: 3**).

Row 9: K0 (0: 0: **0: 1: 1**), [K2tog tbl, inc purlways in next st] 0 (0: 0: **0: 0: 1**) times, P5 (7: 9: **9: 10: 9**), *P2tog, inc knitways in next st, K9, K2tog tbl, inc purlways in next st, P9, rep from * to last 16 (18: 20: **20: 22: 24**) sts, P2tog, inc knitways in next st, K9, K2tog tbl, inc purlways in next st, P1 (3: 5: **5: 7: 9**).

Row 10: K3 (5: 7: **7: 9: 11**), P12, *K12, P12, rep from * to last 6 (8: 10: **10: 12: 14**) sts, K6 (8: 10: **10: 12: 12**), P0 (0: 0: **0: 0: 2**).

Row 11: [K2tog tbl, inc purlways in next st] 0 (0: 0: **0: 0: 1**) times, P4 (6: 8: **8: 10: 9**), *P2tog, inc knitways in next st, K9, K2tog tbl, inc purlways in next st, P9, rep from * to last 17 (19: 21: **21: 23: 25**) sts, P2tog, inc knitways in next st, K9, K2tog tbl, inc purlways in next st, P2 (4: 6: **6: 8: 10**).

Row 12: K4 (6: 8: **8: 10: 12**), P12, *K12, P12, rep from * to last 5 (7: 9: **9: 11: 13**) sts, K5 (7: 9: **9: 11: 12**), P0 (0: 0: **0: 0: 1**).

Row 13: K0 (0: 0: **0: 0: 1**), P3 (5: 7: **7: 9: 10**), *P2tog, inc knitways in next st, K9, K2tog tbl, inc purlways in next st, P9, rep from * to last 18 (20: 22: **22: 24: 26**) sts, P2tog, inc knitways in next st, K9, K2tog tbl, inc purlways in next st, P3 (5: 7: **7: 9: 11**).

Row 14: P0 (0: 0: **0: 0: 1**), K5 (7: 9: **9: 11: 12**), P12, *K12, P12, rep from * to last 4 (6: 8: **8: 10: 12**) sts, K4 (6: 8: **8: 10: 12**).

Row 15: P2 (4: 6: **6: 8: 10**), *P2tog, inc knitways in next st, K9, K2tog tbl, inc purlways in next st, P9, rep from * to last 19 (21: 23: **23: 25: 27**) sts, P2tog, inc knitways in next st, K9, K2tog tbl, inc purlways in next st, P4 (6: 8: **8: 10: 9**), [P2tog, inc knitways in next st] 0 (0: 0: **0: 0: 1**) times.

Row 16: P0 (0: 0: **0: 0: 2**), K6 (8: 10: **10: 12: 12**), P12, *K12, P12, rep from * to last 3 (5: 7: **7: 9: 11**) sts, K3 (5: 7: **7: 9: 11**).

Row 17: P1 (3: 5: **5: 7: 9**), *P2tog, inc knitways in next st, K9, K2tog tbl, inc purlways in next st, P9, rep from * to last 20 (22: 24: **24: 26: 28**) sts, P2tog, inc knitways in next st, K9, K2tog tbl, inc purlways in next st, P5 (7: 9: **9: 11: 9**), [P2tog, inc knitways in next st, K1] 0 (0: 0: **0: 0: 1**) times.

Row 18: P0 (0: 0: **0: 1: 3**), K7 (9: 11: **11: 12: 12**), P12, *K12, P12, rep from * to last 2 (4: 6: **6: 8: 10**) sts, K2 (4: 6: **6: 8: 10**).

Row 19: P0 (2: 4: **4: 6: 8**), *P2tog, inc knitways in next st, K9, K2tog tbl, inc purlways in next st, P9, rep from * to last 21

(23: 25: **25: 27: 29**) sts, P2tog, inc knitways in next st, K9, K2tog tbl, inc purlways in next st, P6 (8: 10: **10: 9: 9**), [P2tog, inc knitways in next st] 0 (0: 0: **0: 1: 1**) times, K0 (0: 0: **0: 0: 2**).

Row 20: P0 (0: 0: **0: 2: 4**), K8 (10: 12: **12: 12: 12**), P12, *K12, P12, rep from * to last 1 (3: 5: **5: 7: 9**) sts, K1 (3: 5: **5: 7: 9**).

Row 21: P1 (1: 3: **3: 5: 7**), [P2tog, inc knitways in next st] 0 (1: 1: **1: 1: 1**) times, K10 (9: 9: **9: 9: 9**), *K2tog tbl, inc purlways in next st, P9, P2tog, inc knitways in next st, K9, rep from * to last 10 (12: 14: **14: 16: 18**) sts, K2tog tbl, inc purlways in next st, P7 (9: 11: **11: 9: 9**), [P2tog, inc knitways in next st] 0 (0: 0: **0: 1: 1**) times, K0 (0: 0: **0: 1: 3**).

Row 22: P0 (0: 1: **1: 3: 5**), K9 (11: 12: **12: 12: 12**), *P12, K12, rep from * to last 12 (14: 16: **16: 18: 20**) sts, P12, K0 (2: 4: **4: 6: 8**).

Row 23: P0 (0: 2: **2: 4: 6**), [P2tog, inc knitways in next st] 0 (1: 1: **1: 1: 1**) times, K10 (9: 9: **9: 9: 9**), *K2tog tbl, inc purlways in next st, P9, P2tog, inc knitways in next st, K9, rep from * to last 11 (13: 15: **15: 17: 19**) sts, K2tog tbl, inc purlways in next st, P8 (10: 9: **9: 9: 9**), [P2tog, inc knitways in next st] 0 (0: 1: **1: 1: 1**) times, K0 (0: 0: **0: 2: 4**).

Row 24: P0 (0: 2: **2: 4: 6**), K10 (12: 12: **12: 12: 12**), *P12, K12, rep from * to last 11 (13: 15: **15: 17: 19**) sts, P11 (12: 12: **12: 12: 12**), K0 (1: 3: **3: 5: 7**).

Row 25: P0 (1: 1: **1: 3: 5**), [P2tog, inc knitways in next st] 0 (0: 1: **1: 1: 1**) times, K9 (10: 9: **9: 9: 9**), *K2tog tbl, inc purlways in next st, P9, P2tog, inc knitways in next st, K9, rep from * to last 12 (14: 16: **16: 18: 20**) sts, K2tog tbl, inc purlways in next st, P9 (11: 9: **9: 9: 9**), [P2tog, inc knitways in next st] 0 (0: 1: **1: 1: 1**) times, K0 (0: 1: **1: 3: 5**).

Row 26: P0 (1: 3: **3: 5: 7**), K11 (12: 12: **12: 12: 12**), *P12, K12, rep from * to last 10 (12: 14: **14: 16: 18**) sts, P10 (12: 12: **12: 12: 12**), K0 (0: 2: **2: 4: 6**).

Row 27: P0 (0: 0: **0: 2: 4**), [P2tog, inc knitways in next st] 0 (0: 1: **1: 1: 1**) times, K8 (10: 9: **9: 9: 9**), *K2tog tbl, inc purlways in next st, P9, P2tog, inc knitways in next st, K9, rep from * to last 13 (15: 17: **17: 19: 21**) sts, K2tog tbl, inc purlways in next st, P10 (9: 9: **9: 9: 9**), [P2tog, inc knitways in next st] 0 (1: 1: **1: 1: 1**) times, K0 (0: 2: **2: 4: 6**).

Row 28: P0 (2: 4: **4: 6: 8**), K12, *P12, K12, rep from * to last 9 (11: 13: **13: 15: 17**) sts, P9 (11: 12: **12: 12: 12**), K0 (0: 1: **1: 3: 5**).

Row 29: P0 (0: 1: **1: 1: 3**), [P2tog, inc knitways in next st] 0 (0: 0: **0: 1: 1**) times, K7 (9: 10: **10: 9: 9**), *K2tog tbl, inc purlways in next st, P9, P2tog, inc knitways in next st, K9, rep from * to last 14 (16: 18: **18: 20: 22**) sts, K2tog tbl, inc purlways in next st, P11 (9: 9: **9: 9: 9**), [P2tog, inc knitways in next st] 0 (1: 1: **1: 1: 1**) times, K0 (1: 3: **3: 5: 7**).

Row 30: P1 (3: 5: **5: 7: 9**), K12, *P12, K12, rep from * to last 8 (10: 12: **12: 14: 16**) sts, P8 (10: 12: **12: 12: 12**), K0 (0: 0: **0: 2: 4**).

Row 31: P0 (0: 0: **0: 0: 2**), [P2tog, inc knitways in next st] 0 (0: 0: **0: 1: 1**) times,

K6 (8: 10: **10: 9:**°, *K2tog tbl, inc purlways in next st, P9, P2tog, inc knitways in next st, K9, rep from * to last 15 (17: 19: **19: 21: 23**) sts, K2tog tbl, inc purlways in next st, P9, P2tog, inc knitways in next st, K0 (2: 4: **4: 6: 8**).

Row 32: P2 (4: 6: **6: 8: 10**), K12, *P12, K12, rep from * to last 7 (9: 11: **11: 13: 15**) sts, P7 (9: 11: **11: 12: 12**), K0 (0: 0: **0: 1: 3**).

Row 33: P0 (0: 0: **0: 1: 1**), [P2tog, inc knitways in next st] 0 (0: 0: **0: 0: 1**) times, K5 (7: 9: **9: 10: 9**), *K2tog tbl, inc purlways in next st, P9, P2tog, inc knitways in next st, K9, rep from * to last 16 (18: 20: **20: 22: 24**) sts, K2tog tbl, inc purlways in next st, P9, P2tog, inc knitways in next st, K1 (3: 5: **5: 7: 9**).

Row 34: P3 (5: 7: **7: 9: 11**), K12, *P12, K12, rep from * to last 6 (8: 10: **10: 12: 14**) sts, P6 (8: 10: **10: 12: 12**), K0 (0: 0: **0: 0: 2**).

Row 35: [P2tog, inc knitways in next st] 0 (0: 0: **0: 0: 1**) times, K4 (6: 8: **8: 10: 9**), *K2tog tbl, inc purlways in next st, P9, P2tog, inc knitways in next st, K9, rep from * to last 17 (19: 21: **21: 23: 25**) sts, K2tog tbl, inc purlways in next st, P9, P2tog, inc knitways in next st, K2 (4: 6: **6: 8: 10**).

Row 36: P4 (6: 8: **8: 10: 12**), K12, *P12, K12, rep from * to last 5 (7: 9: **9: 11: 13**) sts, P5 (7: 9: **9: 11: 12**), K0 (0: 0: **0: 0: 1**).

Row 37: P0 (0: 0: **0: 0: 1**), K3 (5: 7: **7: 9: 10**), *K2tog tbl, inc purlways in next st, P9, P2tog, inc knitways in next st, K9, rep from * to last 18 (20: 22: **22: 24: 26**) sts, K2tog tbl, inc purlways in next st, P9, P2tog, inc knitways in next st, K3 (5: 7: **7: 9: 11**).

Row 38: K0 (0: 0: **0: 0: 1**), P5 (7: 9: **9: 11: 12**), K12, *P12, K12, rep from * to last 4 (6: 8: **8: 10: 12**) sts, P4 (6: 8: **8: 10: 12**).

Row 39: K2 (4: 6: **6: 8: 10**), *K2tog tbl, inc purlways in next st, P9, P2tog, inc knitways in next st, K9, rep from * to last 19 (21: 23: **23: 25: 27**) sts, K2tog tbl, inc purlways in next st, P9, P2tog, inc knitways in next st, K4 (6: 8: **8: 10: 9**), [K2tog tbl, inc purlways in next st] 0 (0: 0: **0: 0: 1**) times.

Row 40: K0 (0: 0: **0: 0: 2**), P6 (8: 10: **10: 12: 12**), K12, *P12, K12, rep from * to last 3 (5: 7: **7: 9: 11**) sts, P3 (5: 7: **7: 9: 11**).

Row 41: K1 (3: 5: **5: 7: 9**), *K2tog tbl, inc purlways in next st, P9, P2tog, inc knitways in next st, K9, rep from * to last 20 (22: 24: **24: 26: 28**) sts, K2tog tbl, inc purlways in next st, K5 (7: 9: **9: 11: 9**), [K2tog tbl, inc purlways in next st, P1] 0 (0: 0: **0: 0: 1**) times.

Row 42: K0 (0: 0: **0: 1: 3**), P7 (9: 11: **11: 12: 12**), K12, *P12, K12, rep from * to last 2 (4: 6: **6: 8: 10**) sts, P2 (4: 6: **6: 8: 10**).

Row 43: K0 (2: 4: **4: 6: 8**), *K2tog tbl, inc purlways in next st, P9, P2tog, inc knitways in next st, K9, rep from * to last 21 (23: 25: **25: 27: 29**) sts, K2tog tbl, inc purlways in next st, P9, P2tog, inc knitways in next st, K6 (8: 10: **10: 9: 9**), [K2tog tbl, inc purlways in next st] 0 (0: 0: **0: 1: 1**) times, P0 (0: 0: **0: 0: 2**).

Row 44: K0 (0: 0: **0: 2: 4**), P8 (10: 12:

12: 12: 12**), K12, *P12, K12, rep from * to last 1 (3: 5: **5: 7: 9**) sts, P1 (3: 5: **5: 7: 9**).

Row 45: K1 (1: 3: **3: 5: 7**), [K2tog tbl, inc purlways in next st] 0 (1: 1: **1: 1: 1**) times, P10 (9: 9: **9: 9: 9**), *P2tog, inc knitways in next st, K9, K2tog tbl, inc purlways in next st, P9, rep from * to last 10 (12: 14: **14: 16: 18**) sts, P2tog, inc knitways in next st, K7 (9: 11: **11: 9: 9**), [K2tog tbl, inc purlways in next st] 0 (0: 0: **0: 1: 1**) times, P0 (0: 0: **0: 1: 3**).

Row 46: K0 (0: 1: **1: 3: 5**), P9 (11: 12: **12: 12: 12**), *K12, P12, rep from * to last 12 (14: 16: **16: 18: 20**) sts, K12, P0 (2: 4: **4: 6: 8**).

Row 47: K0 (0: 2: **2: 4: 6**), [K2tog tbl, inc purlways in next st] 0 (1: 1: **1: 1: 1**) times, P10 (9: 9: **9: 9: 9**), *P2tog, inc knitways in next st, K9, K2tog tbl, inc purlways in next st, P9, rep from * to last 11 (13: 15: **15: 17: 19**) sts, P2tog, inc knitways in next st, K8 (10: 9: **9: 9: 9**), [K2tog tbl, inc purlways in next st] 0 (0: 1: **1: 1: 1**) times, P0 (0: 0: **0: 2: 4**).

Row 48: K0 (0: 2: **2: 4: 6**), P10 (12: 12: **12: 12: 12**), *K12, P12, rep from * to last 11 (13: 15: **15: 17: 19**) sts, K11 (12: 12: **12: 12: 12**), P0 (1: 3: **3: 5: 7**).

These 48 rows form patt.
Cont in patt until back measures 46 cm, ending with a WS row.

Shape armholes
Keeping patt correct, cast off 4 sts at beg of next 2 rows.
85 (89: 93: **93: 97: 101**) sts.
Dec 1 st at each end of next 5 rows, then on foll 3 alt rows.
69 (73: 77: **77: 81: 85**) sts.
Cont without further shaping until armholes measure 25.5 cm, ending with a WS row.

Shape shoulders and back neck
Keeping patt correct, cast off 6 (7: 8: **7: 8: 9**) sts at beg of next 2 rows.
57 (59: 61: **63: 65: 67**) sts.
Next row (RS): Cast off 6 (7: 8: **7: 8: 9**) sts, patt until there are 11 (11: 11: **12: 12: 12**) sts on right needle and turn, leaving rem sts on a holder.
Work each side of neck separately.
Cast off 4 sts at beg of next row.
Cast off rem 7 (7: 7: **8: 8: 8**) sts.
With RS facing, rejoin yarn to rem sts, cast off centre 23 (23: 23: **25: 25: 25**) sts, patt to end.
Work to match first side, reversing shapings.

FRONT
Work as for back until 22 rows less have been worked before start of shoulder shaping, thus ending with a WS row.

Shape neck
Next row (RS): patt 29 (31: 33: **33: 35: 37**) and turn, leave rem sts on a holder.
Work each side of neck separately.
Cast off 4 sts at beg of next row.
25 (27: 29: **29: 31: 33**) sts.
Dec 1 st at neck edge on next 1 (1: 1: **3: 3: 3**) rows, then on foll 3 (3: 3: **2: 2: 2**) alt rows. 21 (23: 25: **24: 26: 28**) sts.
Work 3 rows.
Dec 1 st at neck edge on next and foll 4th row.
19 (21: 23: **22: 24: 26**) sts.
Work 5 rows, thus ending after a WS row.

Shape shoulder

Cast off 6 (7: 8: **7: 8: 9**) sts at beg of next and foll alt row.

Work 1 row.

Cast off rem 7 (7: 7: **8: 8: 8**) sts.

With RS facing, rejoin yarn to rem sts, cast off centre 11 sts, patt to end.

Work to match first side, reversing shapings.

SLEEVES (both alike)

Cast on 49 (49: 49: **53: 53: 53**) sts using 4¹/₂mm (US 7) needles.

Row 1 (RS): P4, P2tog, inc knitways in next st, K9, K2tog tbl, inc purlways in next st, P9, P2tog, inc knitways in next st, K9, K2tog tbl, inc purlways in next st, P6 (6: 6: **10: 10: 10**).

Row 2: K8 (8: 8: **12: 12: 12**), P12, K12, P12, K5.

Row 3: P3, P2tog, inc knitways in next st, K9, K2tog tbl, inc purlways in next st, P9, P2tog, inc knitways in next st, K9, K2tog tbl, inc purlways in next st, P7 (7: 7: **11: 11: 11**).

Row 4: P0 (0: 0: **1: 1: 1**), K9 (9: 9: 12: 12: 12), P12, K12, P12, K4.

These 4 rows set position of patt as for back. Keeping patt correct, cont in patt, shaping sides by inc 1 st at each end of 38th row (from beg of patt) and every foll 6th (6th: 6th: **8th: 8th: 8th**) row until there are 71 (71: 71: **81: 81: 81**) sts, taking inc sts into patt. (**Note**: increases are worked on **WS** rows.)

Ladies sizes only

Inc 1 st at each end of every foll 8th row (from previous inc) until there are 81 sts.

All sizes

Cont without further shaping until sleeve measures 53.5 (53.5: 53.5: **58.5: 58.5: 58.5**) cm, ending with a WS row.

Shape top

Keeping patt correct, cast off 4 sts at beg of next 2 rows. 73 sts.

Dec 1 st at each end of next and foll 4 alt rows. 63 sts.

Dec 1 st at each end of next 3 rows.

Cast off rem 57 sts loosely and evenly.

MAKING UP

PRESS all pieces as described on the information page.

Join right shoulder seam using back stitch.

Sweater with polo neck
Neck border

With RS facing and using 4¹/₂mm (US 7) needles, pick up and knit 18 sts down left front neck, 11 sts across centre front, 18 sts up right front neck and 33 sts across back neck. 80 sts.

Row 1 (WS of sweater, RS of neck border): (K4, P4) 10 times.

Row 2: (K4, P4) 10 times.

Rep last 2 rows for 20 cm.

Cast off loosely and evenly.

Sweater with hood
Left hood

Cast on 8 sts using 4¹/₂mm (US 7) needles.

Beg with a K row, work 3 rows in st st, casting on 4 sts at beg of 3rd row. 12 sts.

Row 4 (WS): K1, P10.

Row 5: Cast on 4 sts, P1, P2tog, inc knitways in next st, K11, P1. 16 sts.

Row 6: K2, P12, K2.

Row 7: Cast on and P 4 sts, P2tog, inc knitways in next st, K9, K2tog tbl, inc purlways in next st, P1. 20 sts.

Row 8: K3, P12, K5.

Row 9: Cast on and P 4 sts, P3, P2tog, inc knitways in next st, K9, K2tog tbl, inc purlways in next st, P2. 24 sts.

Row 10: K4, P12, K8.

These 10 rows set position of patt. Keeping patt correct and taking inc sts into patt, proceed as folls:

Cast on 4 sts at beg of next row. 28 sts.

Work 1 row.

Cast on 4 sts at beg and dec 1 st at end (front opening edge) of next row. 31 sts.

Work 1 row.

Cast on 4 sts at beg of next row. 35 sts.

Place marker at beg of last row to denote base of centre back hood seam.

Work 5 rows, thus ending with a WS row.

Inc 1 st at back edge (beg) of next and 5 foll 6th rows **and at same time** dec 1 st at front opening edge (end) of every foll 12th row from previous dec. 38 sts.

Inc 1 st at back edge **only** of every foll 6th row from previous inc until there are 40 sts.

Work 37 rows, thus ending with a WS row.

Dec 1 st at back edge of next and foll 4 alt rows, then on foll 4 rows, thus ending with a RS row. 31 sts.

Cast off 8 sts at beg and dec 1 st at end of next row.

Cast off rem 22 sts.

Right hood

Cast on 8 sts using 4¹/₂mm (US 7) needles.

Row 1 (RS): Purl.

Row 2: Cast on and P 4 sts, K8. 12 sts.

Row 3: P6, P2tog, inc knitways in next st, K3.

Row 4: Cast on and P 4 sts, P5, K7. 16 sts.

Row 5: P5, P2tog, inc knitways in next st, K8.

Row 6: Cast on 4 sts, K2, P12, K6. 20 sts.

Row 7: P4, P2tog, inc knitways in next st, K9, K2tog tbl, inc purlways in next st, P1.

Row 8: Cast on and K 4 sts, K3, P12, K5. 24 sts.

Row 9: P3, P2tog, inc knitways in next st, K9, K2tog tbl, inc purlways in next st, P6.

Row 10: Cast on and K 4 sts, K8, P12, K4. 28 sts.

These 10 rows set position of patt. Keeping patt correct and taking inc sts into patt, proceed as folls:

Work 1 row.

Cast on 4 sts at beg of next row. 32 sts.

Dec 1 st at beg (front opening edge) of next row. 31 sts.

Cast on 4 sts at beg of next row. 35 sts.

Place marker at beg of last row to denote base of centre back hood seam.

Work 6 rows, thus ending with a WS row.

Inc 1 st at back edge (end) of next and 5 foll 6th rows **and at same time** dec 1 st at front opening edge (beg) of every foll 12th row from previous dec. 38 sts.

Inc 1 st at back edge **only** of every foll 6th row from previous inc until there are 40 sts.

Work 37 rows, thus ending with a WS row.

Dec 1 st at back edge of next and foll 4 alt rows, then on foll 3 rows, thus ending with a WS row. 32 sts.

Cast off 8 sts at beg and dec 1 st at end of next row. 23 sts.

Dec 1 st at beg of next row.

Cast off rem 22 sts.

Join centre back hood seam above markers.

Hood edging

With RS facing and using 4¹/₂mm (US 7) needles, beg at original cast on edge, pick up and knit 60 sts up right front opening edge of hood to seam, then 60 sts down left front opening edge to original cast on edge. 120 sts.

Knit 2 rows.

Cast off knitways.

Sew hood to neck, placing hood seam at centre back and with hood edging meeting at centre front.

Both sweaters

See information page for finishing instructions.

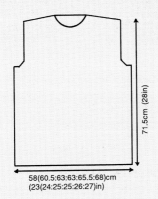

58(60.5:63:63:65.5:68)cm
(23(24:25:25:26:27)in)

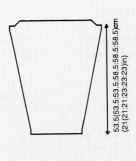

53.5(53.5:53.5:58.5:58.5:58.5)cm
(21(21:21:23:23:23)in)

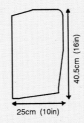

40.5cm (16in)

25cm (10in)

71.5cm (28in)

Design number 15

Gem

KIM HARGREAVES

YARNS
Rowan Chunky Cotton Chenille
2   x   100gm
(Photographed in 379 Chocolate)

NEEDLES
1 pair 4mm (no 8) (US 6) needles

PETERSHAM RIBBON - 4 cm (1¹/₂ ins)
wide, length to fit comfortably around head,
allowing 2 cm for joining.

TENSION
Based on a st st tension of 16 sts and 24 rows
to 10 cm using 4¹/₂mm (US 7) needles.

Measurement To fit average size adult.

MAIN SECTION
Cast on 145 sts using 4mm (US 6) needles.
Row 1 (RS): Knit.
Row 2: Purl.
Rows 3 and 4: Knit.
Row 5: P1, *P2tog, P16, rep from * to
end. 137 sts.
Row 6: Knit.
Beg with a K row, now work in st st as folls:
Work 2 rows.
Row 9: K1, *K2tog, K15, rep from * to
end. 129 sts.
Work 3 rows.
Row 13: K1, *K2tog, K14, rep from * to
end. 121 sts.
Work 3 rows.
Row 17: K1, *K2tog, K13, rep from * to
end. 113 sts.
Work 3 rows.
Row 21: K1, *K2tog, K12, rep from * to
end. 105 sts.
Work 1 row, thus ending with a WS row.
Place markers at both ends of last row.
Beg with a P row, work 3 rows in rev st st.
Beg with a P row, work 3 rows in st st.
Rep last 6 rows 6 times more.
Cast off loosely and evenly.

CROWN
Cast on 105 sts using 4mm (US 6) needles.
Row 1 (RS): Knit.
Row 2 and every foll alt row: Purl.
Row 3: K1, *K2tog, K11, rep from * to
end. 97 sts.
Row 5: K1, *K2tog, K10, rep from * to
end. 89 sts.
Row 7: K1, *K2tog, K9, rep from * to end.
81 sts.
Row 9: K1, *K2tog, K8, rep from * to end.
73 sts.
Row 11: K1, *K2tog, K7, rep from * to
end. 65 sts.
Row 13: K1, *K2tog, K6, rep from * to
end. 57 sts.
Row 15: K1, *K2tog, K5, rep from * to
end. 49 sts.
Row 17: K1, *K2tog, K4, rep from * to
end. 41 sts.
Row 19: K1, *K2tog, K3, rep from * to
end. 33 sts.
Row 21: K1, *K2tog, K2, rep from * to
end. 25 sts.
Row 23: K1, *K2tog, K1, rep from * to
end. 17 sts.
Row 25: K1, *K2tog, rep from * to end.
Break yarn and thread through rem 9 sts.
Pull up tight and fasten off securely.

MAKING UP
Join crown seam. Join back seam of main
section. Holding pieces WS facing, join
crown to main section using back stitch (so
that seam forms ridge on RS). Join ends of
petersham to form a ring. Sew petersham
inside hat by slip stitching lower edge to sts of
marked row, easing hat to fit.

Design number 16

Rupert

KIM HARGREAVES

YARNS
Rowan Fine Cotton Chenille
One colour version
4   x   50gm
(Photographed in 416 Marsh)

Striped version

A	Privet	410	1	x	50gm
B	Naval	417	1	x	50gm
C	Plum	409	1	x	50gm
D	Mousse	418	1	x	50gm
E	Black	413	1	x	50gm

NEEDLES
1 pair 3mm (no 11) (US 2/3) needles

TENSION
22 sts and 36 rows to 10 cm measured over
rib slightly stretched using 3mm (US 2/3)
needles.

Measurement
23 cm (9 ins) wide.
202.5 (80 ins) long.

Colour note: References to yarn A, B, C,
D and E are for striped version only. For one
colour version, use same colour throughout.

SCARF
Cast on 50 sts using 3mm (US 2/3) needles
and yarn A.
Row 1 (RS): K2, *P2, K2, rep from * to
end.
Row 2: P2, *K2, P2, rep from * to end.
Last 2 rows form rib patt.
Cont in patt until scarf measures 40.5 cm.
Break off yarn A and join in yarn B.
Cont in patt until scarf measures 81 cm.
Break off yarn B and join in yarn C.
Cont in patt until scarf measures 121.5 cm.
Break off yarn C and join in yarn D.
Cont in patt until scarf measures 162 cm.
Break off yarn D and join in yarn E.
Cont in patt until scarf measures 202.5 cm.
Cast off loosely and evenly.

MAKING UP
STEAM PRESS gently to set the stitches.
Fringing
*Cut 4 strands of yarn A, each 25 cm long,
and fold in half. Insert a crochet hook from
WS between first 2 sts of cast on edge and
bring looped ends of yarn through to WS of
scarf. Hook loose ends through loop and pull
to knot in place.
Rep from * along cast on edge, working into
every 4th stitch.
Using yarn E, make fringe along cast off
edge in same way.

Design number 17

Bella

KIM HARGREAVES

YARNS
Rowan Fine Cotton Chenille
2   x   50gm
(Photographed in 415 Parched)

NEEDLES
1 pair 3³/₄mm (no 9) (US 5) needles

TENSION
20 sts and 24 rows to 10 cm measured over patt using 3³/₄mm (US 5) needles.

Measurement
24 cm (9¹/₂ ins) wide. 120 cm (47 ins) long.

SCARF
Cast on 48 sts using 3³/₄mm (US 5) needles.
Beg with a K row, work 4 rows in st st.
Now work in bobble patt as folls:
Row 1 (WS): *K2tog, (yfwd) twice, K2tog, rep from * to end.
Row 2: *K1, (K1, P1) into double (yfwd) of previous row, K1, rep from * to end.
Row 3: K2, *K2tog, (yfwd) twice, K2tog, rep from * to last 2 sts, K2.
Row 4: K2, *K1, (K1, P1) into double (yfwd) of previous row, K1, rep from * to last 2 sts, K2.
Rep last 4 rows until scarf measures 119 cm.
Beg with a K row, work 4 rows in st st.
Cast off loosely and evenly.

Design number 18

Bilberry Cushion

KIM HARGREAVES

YARNS
Rowan Chunky Cotton Chenille
2   x   100gm
(Photographed in 356 Aubergine)

NEEDLES
1 pair 4¹/₂mm (no 7) (US 7) needles

TENSION
16 sts and 24 rows to 10 cm measured over patt using 4¹/₂mm (US 7) needles.

Measurement
To fit 41 cm (16 ins) square cushion pad.

SPECIAL ABBREVIATIONS
MB = Make bobble as folls: (K1, P1, K1, P1, K1) all into next st, turn, K5, turn, K5, lift 2nd, 3rd, 4th and 5th st over first st.

KNITTED PANEL
Cast on 61 sts using 4¹/₂mm (US 7) needles.
Beg with a K row, work 4 rows in st st.
Now work in bobble patt as folls:
Row 1 (RS): K2, *MB, K3, rep from * to last 3 sts, MB, K2.
Beg with a P row, work 3 rows in st st.
Row 5: K4, *MB, K3, rep from * to last st, K1.
Beg with a P row, work 3 rows in st st.
Last 8 rows form bobble patt.
Cont in patt until work measures approx 40 cm, ending after patt row 4 or 8.
Beg with a K row, work 2 rows in st st.
(Work should now measure 41 cm.)
Cast off loosely and evenly.

MAKING UP
Cut 45cm (18 ins) square of backing fabric. Lay knitted section onto fabric, RS facing, and stitch together along 3 sides, turn RS out and insert cushion pad. Slip stitch together edges on 4th side.

Design number 19

Lush Cushion

KIM HARGREAVES

YARNS
Rowan Chunky Cotton Chenille
2   x   100gm
(Photographed in 384 Lily)

NEEDLES
1 pair 4¹/₂mm (no 7) (US 7) needles
Cable needle

TENSION
16 sts and 24 rows to 10 cm measured over st st using 4¹/₂mm (US 7) needles.

Measurement
To fit 41 cm (16 ins) square cushion pad.

SPECIAL ABBREVIATIONS
C6F = Cable 6 front Slip next 3 sts onto cable needle and hold at front, K3, then K3 from cable needle.
C6B = Cable 6 back Slip next 3 sts onto cable needle and hold at back, K3, then K3 from cable needle.

KNITTED PANEL
Cast on 53 sts using 4¹/₂mm (US 7) needles.
Row 1 (RS) (inc): K1, inc once in every st to last st, K1. 104 sts.
Row 2: K1, P to last st, K1.

Lush

Bilberry

Now work in cable patt as folls:
Row 1 (RS): K1, (C6B) to last st, K1.
Row 2 and every foll alt row: K1, P to last st, K1.
Row 3: Knit.
Row 5: Knit.
Row 7: K4, (C6F) to last 4 sts, K4.
Row 9: Knit.
Row 11: Knit.
Row 12: As row 2.
Last 12 rows form cable patt.
Cont in patt until work measures 41 cm, ending after patt row 6 or 12.
Cast off loosely and evenly.

MAKING UP
Cut 45cm (18 ins) square of backing fabric. Lay knitted section onto fabric, RS facing, and stitch together along 3 sides, turn RS out and insert cushion pad. Slip stitch together edges on 4th side.

Design number 20

Glow Cushion and Blanket

KIM HARGREAVES

YARNS
Rowan Chunky Cotton Chenille
Cushion Cover   2   x   100gm
(Photographed in 386 Lavender and 383 Parchment)

One Colour Blanket   18   x   100gm
(Not photographed)

Five Colour Blanket

A Aubergine	356	3	x	100gm
B Blackcurrant	381	5	x	100gm
C Chocolate	379	5	x	100gm
D French Mustard	363	3	x	100gm
E Elephant	348	3	x	100gm

NEEDLES
1 pair 4¹/₂mm (no 7) (US 7) needles

TENSION
16 sts and 24 rows to 10 cm measured over st st using 4¹/₂mm (US 7) needles.

Measurement
To fit 41 cm (16 ins) square cushion pad.
Blanket 122 cm (48 ins) by 162.5 cm (64 ins).

Cushion cover
KNITTED PANEL (make 4)
Cast on 1 st using 4¹/₂mm (US 7) needles.
Row 1 (RS): Inc in st. 2 sts.
Row 2: Inc in first st, P1. 3 sts.
Beg with a P row, work 3 rows in reverse st st, inc 1 st at beg of every row. 6 sts.
Beg with a P row, work 3 rows in st st, inc 1 st at beg of every row. 9 sts.
Last 6 rows form patt.
Keeping patt correct, work 38 rows, inc 1 st at beg of every row. 47 sts.
Place markers at both ends of last row.
Still keeping patt correct, now dec 1 st at beg of every row until 1 st remains.
Fasten off.

Blanket
Make 48 knitted panels in same way as for cushion cover - for five colour version, make 8 using yarn A, 12 using yarn B, 12 using yarn C, 8 using yarn D and 8 using yarn E.

MAKING UP
Cushion cover
Join knitted panels to form a square, joining panels from cast on edge to markers. Pin out to form a 41 cm (16 ins) square and press. Cut 45cm (18 ins) square of backing fabric. Lay knitted section onto fabric, RS facing, and stitch together along 3 sides, turn RS out and insert cushion pad. Slip stitch together edges on 4th side.

Blanket
Join sets of 4 knitted panels to form a larger square, joining panels from cast on edge to markers. Pin out to form a 41 cm (16 ins) square and press.
Now join larger squares to form blanket, arranging squares as in diagram below.

B	B	E	E	C	C
B	B	E	E	C	C
C	C	D	D	A	A
C	C	D	D	A	A
E	E	A	A	B	B
E	E	A	A	B	B
B	B	C	C	D	D
B	B	C	C	D	D

Design number 21

Zebra Cushion

KIM HARGREAVES

YARNS
Rowan Chunky Cotton Chenille
First colourway

A Parchment	383	1	x	100gm
B Black	367	1	x	100gm

Second colourway

A Chocolate	379	1	x	100gm
B Black	367	1	x	100gm

NEEDLES
1 pair 4¹/₂mm (no 7) (US 7) needles

TENSION
16 sts and 24 rows to 10 cm measured over st st using 4¹/₂mm (US 7) needles.

Measurement
To fit 41 cm (16 ins) square cushion pad.

KNITTED PANEL
Cast on 65 sts using 4¹/₂mm (US 7) needles and yarn A.
Beg and ending rows as indicated and using the **intarsia** technique described on the information page, work 98 rows in patt from body chart of Zebra jacket, design number 1, shown on page 25, which is worked entirely in st st, beg with a K row and thus ending with a WS row.
Cast off loosely and evenly.

MAKING UP
Cut 45cm (18 ins) square of backing fabric. Lay knitted section onto fabric, RS facing, and stitch together along 3 sides, turn RS out and insert cushion pad. Slip stitch together edges on 4th side.

INFORMATION PAGE

KNITTING WITH CHENILLE

Getting the tension correct when knitting with chenille can be difficult. Knitters often get a **bar** between each stitch making the knitting too open. This is because the pile does not allow the yarn to re-adjust itself on the needles, so the stitch has to be created in a more precise way. If you run your finger tips down a length of chenille you will feel the pile is smoother one way than the other, so when knitting you will find it much easier if the pile is going away from your knitting rather than towards it and also unlike knitting fairisle where you spread your stitches to keep the work elastic, when knitting with chenille keep the stitch just knitted close to the tip of the right hand needle and then work the next stich close up to it.

TENSION

Obtaining the correct tension is perhaps the single factor which can make the difference between a successful garment and a disastrous one. It controls both the shape and size of an article, so any variation, however slight, can distort the finished look of the garment. No-one wants to spend hours and hours making a "skinny rib" when they really want a "sloppy Joe".

You must match the tension given at the **start** of each pattern. We strongly advise that you knit a square in pattern and or stocking stitch (depending on the pattern instruction) of perhaps 5 - 10 more stitches and 5 - 10 more rows than those given in the tension note. Place the finished square on a flat surface and measure the central area. If you have too many stitches to 10cm try again using thicker needles, if you have too few stitches to 10cm try again using finer needles. Once you have achieved the correct tension your garment will be knitted to the measurements given in the pattern.

SIZE NOTE

The instructions are given for the smallest size. Where they vary, work the figures in brackets for the larger sizes. One set of figures refers to all sizes. For ease in reading charts it may be helpful to have the chart enlarged at a printers and then to outline the size you intend to knit on the chart.

CHART NOTE

Some of the patterns in the book are worked from charts. Each square on a chart represents a stitch and each line of squares a row of knitting. When working from the charts, read odd rows (K) from right to left and even rows (P) from left to right, unless otherwise stated. Each colour used is given a different symbol or letter and these are shown in the **materials** section, or in the **key** alongside the chart of each pattern.

KNITTING WITH COLOUR

Intarsia: The simplest way to do this is to cut short lengths of yarn for each motif or block of colour used in a row. Then joining in the various colours at the appropriate point on the row, link one colour to the next by twisting them around each other where they meet on the wrong side to avoid gaps. All ends can then either be darned along the colour join lines, as each motif is completed or then can be "knitted-in" to the fabric of the knitting as each colour is worked into the pattern. This is done in much the same way as "weaving-in" yarns when working the Fairisle technique and does save time darning-in ends.

ALL ribs should be knitted to a firm tension, for some knitters it may be necessary to use a smaller needle. In order to prevent sagging in cuffs and welts we suggest you use a "knitting-in" elastic.

PRESSING

After working for hours knitting a garment, it seems a great pity that many garments are spoiled because so little care is taken in the pressing and finishing. After darning in all the ends, block each piece of knitting. Press each piece, except ribs, gently, using a warm iron over a damp cloth. Take special care to press the edges as this will make the sewing up both easier and neater.

FINISHING INSTRUCTIONS

When stitching the pieces together match the colour patterns very carefully. Use a back stitch for all main knitting seams and an edge to edge stitch for all ribs unless otherwise stated.
Join left shoulder seam using back stitch and neckband seam (where appropriate) using an edge to edge stitch.
Sleeves
Set in sleeves: Set in sleeve easing sleeve head into armhole using back stitch.
Square set in sleeve: Set sleeve head into armhole, the straight sides at top of sleeve to form a neat right-angle to cast off sts at armhole on back and front, using back stitch.
Straight cast off sleeve: Place centre of cast off edge of sleeve to shoulder seam. Sew in sleeve using back stitch using markers as guidelines where applicable.
Join side and sleeve seams using back stitch.
Slip stitch pocket edgings and linings into place.
Sew on buttons to correspond with buttonholes.
After sewing up, press seams and hems. Ribbed welts and neckbands and any areas of garter stitch should not be pressed.

= Easy, straight forward knitting

= Suitable for the average knitter

= For the more experienced knitter

ABBREVIATIONS

K	knit
P	purl
st(s)	stitch(es)
inc	increas(e)(ing)
dec	decreas(e)(ing)
st st	stocking stitch (1 row K, 1 row P)
garter st	garter stitch (K every row)
beg	begin(ning)
foll	following
folls	follows
rem	remain(ing)
rev	revers(e)(ing)
rep	repeat
alt	alternate
cont	continue
patt	pattern
tog	together
mm	millimetres
cm	centimetres
in(s)	inch(es)
RS	right side
WS	wrong side
psso	pass slip stitch over
tbl	through back of loop
sl	slip
M1	make one stitch by picking up horizontal loop before next stitch and knitting into back of it
M1P	make one stitch by picking up horizontal loop before next stitch and purling into back of it
yon	yarn over needle
yfwd	yarn forward
yrn	yarn round needle

Rowan Stockists - United Kingdom & Eire

Names in bold type are Rowan dedicated shops or departments, many offering professional help and mail order facilities

BATH & NORTH EAST SOMERSET
BATH - ROWAN AT STITCH SHOP, 15 The Podium, Northgate. Tel: 01225 481134 Mail Order Access/Visa/American Express
Bath - Kaffe Fassett Designs Limited, 3 Saville Row. Tel: 01225 484215

BRISTOL
BRISTOL - ROWAN AT JOHN LEWIS, The Horsefair. Tel: 0117 9279100

BEDFORDSHIRE
LEIGHTON BUZZARD - ROWAN AT BAH BAH'S, Peacock Mews. Tel: 01525 376456 Mail Order

BERKSHIRE
READING - ROWAN AT HEELAS, Broad Street. Tel: 0118 9 575955
South Ascot - South Ascot Wools, 18 Brockenhurst Road. Tel: 01344 628327a
Windsor - Caleys, 19 High Street. Tel: 01753 863241

BUCKINGHAMSHIRE
AYLESBURY - ROWAN AT BEATTIES, 27 Friars Square. Tel: 01296 399996 Access/Visa
MILTON KEYNES - ROWAN AT JOHN LEWIS, Central Milton Keynes. Tel: 01908 679171

CAMBRIDGESHIRE
CAMBRIDGE - ROWAN AT ROBERT SAYLE, St Andrews Street. Tel: 01223 361292
Peterborough - John Lewis, Queensgate Centre. Tel: 01733 344644

CHESHIRE
ALTRINCHAM - ROWAN AT CREATIVE KNITTING, 27A Oxford Road. Tel: 0161 941 2534 Mail Order Access/Visa 24 Hr Ansphone
Cheadle - John Lewis, Wilmslow Road. Tel: 0161 491 4914

CORNWALL
Penzance - Iriss, 66 Chapel Street. Tel: 01736 366568
St. Ives - Antiques, Buttons & Crafts, 3A Tregenna Hill. Tel: 01736 793713
WADEBRIDGE - ROWAN AT ARTYCRAFTS, 41 Molesworth Street. Tel: 01208 812274

CUMBRIA
Carlisle - Pingouin, 20 Globe Lane. Tel: 01228 20681
PENRITH - ROWAN AT INDIGO, 7 Devonshire Arcade. Tel: 01768 899917 Mail Order Access/Visa
Ulverston - Smith's Court Emporium, Smith's Court. Tel: 01229 582606

DERBYSHIRE
Bakewell - Woollie Pullie, Unit 5, Portland Square. Tel: 01629 812235 Mail Order Access/Visa

DEVON
Braunton - Woolcrafts, 19 Cross Tree Centre. Tel: 01271 815075
PLYMOUTH - ROWAN AT DINGLES, 40-46 Royal Parade. Tel: 01752 266611 Mail Order Access/Visa
Tavistock - Knitting Image, 9 Pepper Street. Tel: 01822 617410
Totnes - Sally Carr Designs, The Yarn Shop, 31 High Street, Tel: 01803 863060

DORSET
Bridport - Harlequin, 76 West Street. Tel: 01308 456449
Christchurch - Honora, 69 High Street. Tel: 01202 486000
Sherborne - Hunters of Sherborne, 4 Tilton Court, Digby Road. Tel: 01935 817722
Wimborne - The Walnut Tree, 1 West Borough. Tel: 01202 840722

DURHAM
Barnard Castle - Castle Fabrics & Crafts, 3 Market Place. Tel: 01833 638412 Mail Order
DARLINGTON - ROWAN AT BINNS, 7 High Row. Tel: 01325 462606 Mail Order Access/Visa

GLOUCESTERSHIRE
CHELTENHAM - ROWAN AT CAVENDISH HOUSE, The Promenade. Tel: 01242 521300 Mail Order Access/Visa

HAMPSHIRE
ALRESFORD - ROWAN AT DESIGNER KNITS, 14 West Street. Tel: 01962 735151
Lymington - Honee Bee, 7 Gosport Street. Tel: 01590 674986
Southampton - Tyrrell & Green, Above Bar. Tel: 01703 227711
Southsea - Knight & Lee, Palmerston Road. Tel: 01705 827511
Twyford - Riverside Yarns, Cockscombe Farm, Watley Lane. Tel: 01962 714380
Winchester - C & H Fabrics, 8 High Street. Tel: 01962 843355

HERTFORDSHIRE
Boreham Wood - The Wool Shop, 92 Shenley Road. Tel: 0181 905 2499 Mail Order
Harpenden - In Stitches, 12 Leyton Road. Tel: 01582 769011 Access/Visa/Amex
WATFORD - ROWAN AT TREWINS, The Harlequin, High Street. Tel: 01923 244266
WELWYN GARDEN CITY - ROWAN AT JOHN LEWIS. Tel: 01707 323456

KENT
Canterbury - C & H Fabrics, 2 St. George's Street. Tel: 01227 459760
Edenbridge - Burghesh Court, 3 The Village, Chiddingstone. Tel: 01892 870326
Maidstone - C & H Fabrics, 68 Week Street. Tel: 01622 762054
Rochester - **ROWAN AT Francis Iles**, 73 High Street. Tel: 01634 843082 Mail Order Access/Visa
Tunbridge Wells - C & H Fabrics, 113/115 Mount Pleasant. Tel: 01892 522618

LANCASHIRE
St Anne's-on-Sea - Kathleen Barnes, 22 The Crescent. Tel/Fax: 01253 724194 Mail Order Access/Visa

LEICESTERSHIRE
Oakham - The Wool Centre, 40 Melton Road. Tel: 01572 757574 Mail Order Access/Visa

LONDON - CENTRAL
ROWAN AT HARRODS - 87-135 Brompton Road, Knightsbridge, SW1X 7XL. Tel: 0171 730 1234 Mail Order Access/Visa
ROWAN AT CREATIVITY - 45 New Oxford Street, WC1. Tel: 0171 240 2945 Fax: 0171 240 6030 Mail Order Access/Visa
ROWAN AT COLOURWAY - 112A Westbourne Grove, W2. Tel: 0171 229 1432 Mail Order Access/Visa 24 Hr Ansphone
ROWAN AT LIBERTY - Regent Street, W1. Tel: 0171 734 1234 Mail Order Access/Visa
ROWAN AT JOHN LEWIS - Oxford Street, W1. Tel: 0171 629 7711
ROWAN AT PETER JONES - Sloane Square, SW1. Tel: 0171 730 3434

LONDON - NORTH
ROWAN AT JOHN LEWIS - Brent Cross Shopping Centre, NW4. Tel: 0181 202 6535

LONDON - SOUTH
Needles Wool Shop - Thornton Road, East Sheen SW14. Tel: 0181 878 1592
Creations - 79 Church Road, Barnes SW13. Tel: 0181 563 2970

MERSEYSIDE
LIVERPOOL - ROWAN AT GEORGE HENRY LEE, Basnett Street. Tel: 0151 709 7070
Wirral - Voirrey Embroidery Centre, Brimsgate Hall, Brimsgate. Tel: 0151 342 3514

NORFOLK
CROMER - ROWAN AT COTTAGE YARNS, 2A Mount Street. Tel: 01263 515433 Mail Order Access/Visa
Norwich - Bonds, All Saints Green. Tel: 01603 660021

NORTHUMBERLAND
Corbridge - The Fabric & Tapestry Shop, Sydgate House, Middle Street. Tel: 01434 632902 Mail Order

NOTTINGHAMSHIRE
NOTTINGHAM - ROWAN AT JESSOPS, Victoria Centre. Tel: 0115 9418282

OXFORDSHIRE
Burford - Burford Needlecraft Shop, 117 High Street. Tel: 01993 822136 Mail Order Access/Visa
OXFORD - ROWAN AT ROWAN - 102 Gloucester Green. Tel: 01865 793366 Mail Order Access/Visa 24 Hr Ansphone

SHROPSHIRE
SHREWSBURY - ROWAN AT HOUSE OF NEEDLEWORK, 11 Wyle Cop. Tel: 01743 355533 (Formerly Osa)

SOMERSET
Burnham-on-Sea - The Woolsack, 7 College Street. Tel: 01278 784443
Taunton - Hayes Wools, 150 East Reach. Tel: 01823 284768 Mail Order Access/Visa
Yeovil - Enid's, Wool & Craft Shop, Church Street. Tel: 01935 412421

SUFFOLK
BURY ST EDMUNDS - ROWAN AT JAYCRAFT, 78 St John's Street. Tel: 01284 752982 Mail Order
Ipswich - Spare Moments, 13 Northgate Street. Tel: 01473 259876

STAFFORDSHIRE
Newcastle under Lyme - The Spinning Wheel, 40 High Street. Tel: 01782 630484

SURREY
NR DORKING - ROWAN AT HOLMCROFT SUPPLIES, 186 The Street, Capel. Tel: 01306 711126 Mail Order Access/Visa
GUILDFORD - ROWAN AT ARMY & NAVY, High Street. Tel: 01483 568171 Mail Order Access/Visa
KINGSTON - ROWAN AT JOHN LEWIS, Wood Street. Tel: 0181 547 3000
South Croydon - Knitz 'N' Bitz, 12 Selsdon Road. Tel: 0181 688 7629

EAST SUSSEX
BRIGHTON - ROWAN AT COLOURWORKS, 22 Gardner Street. Tel: 01273 628860 Mail Order Access/Visa
Brighton - C & H Fabrics, 179 Western Road. Tel: 01273 321671
Eastbourne - C & H Fabrics, 82/86 Terminus Road. Tel: 01323 410503
East Hoathley (Nr Uckfield) - The Wool Loft, Upstairs at Clara's, 9 High Street. Tel: 01825 840339 Mail Order
Forest Row - Village Crafts, The Square. Tel: 01342 823238
Lewes - Kangaroo, 70 High Street. Tel: 01273 478554 Access/Visa Mail Order

WEST SUSSEX
ARUNDEL - ROWAN AT DAVIDS NEEDLE-ART, 37 Tarrant Street. Tel: 01903 882761
Chichester - C & H Fabrics, 33/34 North Street. Tel: 01243 783300
PETWORTH - ROWAN AT DAVIDS NEEDLE-ART, Market Square. Tel: 01798 342811
SHOREHAM BY SEA - ROWAN AT SHOREHAM KNITTING, 19 East Street. Tel: 01273 461029 Email: skn@sure-employ.demon.co.uk Mail Order

TEESIDE
Hartlepool - Bobby Davison, 101 Park Road. Tel: 01429 861300

TYNE & WEAR
GATESHEAD - ROWAN AT HOUSE OF FRASER, Metro Centre. Tel: 0191 493 2424 Mail Order Access/Visa
NEWCASTLE UPON TYNE - ROWAN AT BAINBRIDGE, Eldon Square. Tel: 0191 232 5000

WARWICKSHIRE
Warwick - Warwick Wools, 17 Market Place. Tel: 01926 492853

WEST MIDLANDS
BIRMINGHAM - ROWAN AT RACKHAMS, Corporation Street. Tel: 0121 236 3333 Mail Order Access/Visa
WOLVERHAMPTON - ROWAN AT BEATTIES, 71-78 Victoria Street. Tel: 01902 422311 Access/Visa

WILTSHIRE
Calne - Handi Wools, 3 Oxford Road. Tel: 01249 812081
Salisbury - Sarah Miles, Stitches, Cross Keys Chequer. Tel: 01722 411148 Mail Order

WORCESTERSHIRE
Droitwich - Fil D'or, 20 High Street. Tel: 01905 776793

NORTH YORKSHIRE
HELMSLEY - ROWAN AT CRAFT BASICS, 2 Castlegate. Tel: 01439 771300 Mail Order Access/Visa
RIPON - ROWAN AT CATHEDRAL YARNS, 6 Kirkgate. Tel: 01765 604007
Settle - Ancient & Modern, Station Street. Tel: 01729 824298
WHITBY - ROWAN AT BOBBINS, Wesley Hall, Church Street. Tel: 01947 600585 Mail Order Access/Visa Email: bobbins@globalnet.co.uk
YORK - ROWAN AT CRAFT BASICS, 9 Gillygate. Tel: 01904 652840

SOUTH YORKSHIRE
SHEFFIELD - ROWAN AT COLE BROTHERS, Barkers Pool. Tel: 0114 2768511

WEST YORKSHIRE
Hebden Bridge - Attica Fabrics, 2 Commercial Street. Tel: 01422 844327 Mail Order
HOLMFIRTH - ROWAN AT UP COUNTRY, 6 Market Walk. Tel & Fax: 01484 687803 Email: gpaul@upco.u-net.com Mail Order Access/Visa / www.upco.u-net.com/

WALES
Conwy - Ar-y-Gweill, 8 Heol Yr Orsaf, Llanrwst. Tel: 01492 641149
Dyfed - Wool Baa, 33 Blue Street, Carmarthen. Tel: 01267 236734
Fishguard - Melin Tregwynt, 6 High Street. Tel: 01348 872370
St Davids - Melin Tregwynt, 5 Nun Street. Tel: 01437 720386

SCOTLAND
ABERDEEN - ROWAN AT HARLEQUIN, 65 Thistle Street. Tel: 01224 635716 Mail Order Access/Visa
Aberdeen - John Lewis, George Street. Tel: 01224 625000
Castle Douglas - Needlecraft, 201 King Street. Tel: 01556 503606
EDINBURGH - ROWAN AT JOHN LEWIS, St James Centre. Tel: 0131 556 9121
EDINBURGH - ROWAN AT JENNERS, 48 Princes Street. Tel: 0131 225 2442 Mail Order Access/Visa
GLASGOW - ROWAN AT MANDORS, 346 Sauchiehall Street at 1 Scott Street. Tel: 0141 332 7716
East Lothian - Longniddry Post Office, 29a Links Road, Longniddry. Tel: 01875 852894 Mail Order
HELENSBURGH - ROWAN AT ELIZABETH POTTERTON, 42 West Clyde Street. Tel: 01436 671747 Mail Order Access/Visa
Invernesshire - Linda Usher, 50 High Street, Beauly. Tel: 01463 783017
Isle of Arran - Trareoch Craft Shop, Whiting Bay. Tel: 01770 700226
Isle of Skye - Struan Craft Studio, Struan. Tel: 01470 572 284
Lanarkshire - Strands, 8 Bloomgate, Lanark. Tel: 01555 665757 Mail Order Access/Visa
Montrose - Mary Stuart Scott, Lumenart, 20/22 Murray Street. Tel: 01674 675502
Roxburghshire - Floors Castle Garden Centre, Kelso. Tel: 01573 224530

SHETLAND ISLANDS
ROWAN AT WIMBERRY - Gardens, Skeld. Tel: 01595 860371 Mail Order Access/Visa

EIRE
Dublin - Needle Craft Ltd., 27/28 Dawson Street, Dublin 2. Tel: +3531 6772493 Fax: +3531 6771446 Email: ncraft@iol.ie Mail Order Access/Visa / www.ils.ie/needlecraft

ROWAN YARNS, GREEN LANE MILL, HOLMFIRTH, WEST YORKSHIRE, ENGLAND TEL:01484 681881

Rowan Stockists - Overseas

ROWAN DISTRIBUTORS For more information on Overseas Stockists and Mail Order details please contact the Rowan distributor listed under each country
'ROWAN AT ....' stockists who carry a large range of Rowan Yarns

AUSTRALIA
DISTRIBUTOR: MacEwen Enterprises, 1/178 Cherry Lane, Laverton North, Vic 3026, Tel 03 9369 3988/ FreePhone 1800 816 539

Canterbury - ROWAN AT Sunspun, 185 Canterbury Road, VIC 3126. Tel (03) 9830 1609 MAIL ORDER SERVICE AVAILABLE
Lindfield - ROWAN AT Greta's Handcrafts Centre, 321 Pacific Highway, NSW 2070. Tel (02) 9416 2489
Malvern - Wondaflex Yarncraft Centre, 1353 Malvern Road, VIC 3144 Tel (03) 9822 6231
Montrose - Montrose Wool & Craft, Shop 6/926-930, Mt Dandenong Tourist Road, VIC 3765 Tel (03) 9728 6437

AUSTRIA
Wien -ROWAN AT Wolle & Knopfe - Riki Sauberer, Josefstadter Str. 14, A-1080 Tel 1/40 35 735

BELGIUM
DISTRIBUTOR:Pavan, Koningin Astridlaan 78, B9000 Gent Tel (09) 221 8594

Antwerpen - ROWAN AT Lana, Anselmostraat 92, 2018 Tel (03) 238 70 17
Beveren-Waas - Bolleke Wol, Donkvijverstaat 13, Tel (03) 775 26 34
Hasselt - Brelboetiek Hilda, Herkenrodesingel 2, Tel (011) 25 50 71
Nivelles - Artmony, Rue de Levechier 8, 1400 Tel (067) 22 05 29
St-Niklaas - ROWAN AT 't Wolleken, Ankerstraat 28, 9100 Tel (03) 777 64 15
Vorselaar - ROWAN AT 't Allegaartje, Kuiperstraat 22a, Tel (014) 51 64 73
Wetteren - 't Gaerenhuys, Jozef Buyssestraat 9, Tel (09) 366 37 41
Wilsele - ROWAN AT D. Yarns, P Van Langendoncklaan 17, Tel (016) 20 13 81

CANADA
DISTRIBUTOR: Diamond Yarn, 9697 St Laurent, Montreal, Que H3L 2N1 Tel (514) 388-6188 /
Diamond Yarn (Toronto), 155 Martin Ross, Unit 5, Toronto, Ont. M3J 2L9 Tel (416) 736-6111

ALBERTA
Calgary - Gina Brown Holdings, 17,6624 Centre Sr S.E., T2H 0C6 Tel (403) 225-2200
Calgary - Fiber Hut, No1-2614 4th Street N W, T2M 3A1 Tel (403) 230-3822
Edmonton - Knit & Purl, 10412-124 Street, T5N 1R5 Tel (403) 482-2150
Edmonton - Wool Revival, 6513-112 Avenue, T5W 0P1 Tel (403) 471-2749
St Albert - Burwood House, 205 Carnegie Drive T8N 5B2 Tel (403) 459-4828

BRITISH COLUMBIA
Chilliwack - Country Craft Creations, 46291 Yale Road East, V2P 2P7 Tel (604) 792-5434
Duncan - The Loom, R.R. #7,V9L 4W4 Tel (250) 746-5250
Prince George - House of Wool, 1282 N.Nechako Road, V2K 1A6 Tel (250) 562-2803
Richmond - ROWAN AT Craft Cottage, 7577 Elmbridge Way, V6X 2Z8 Tel (604) 278-0313
Richmond - Imagine Craft Co Ltd, 1835-4311 Hazelbridge Way V6X 3V7 Tel (604) 270-9683
Sidney - ROWAN AT In Sheep's Clothing, 9711 5th Street, V8L 2W9 Tel (250) 656-2499
Vancouver - Knit & Stitch, 2419 Marine Drive, V7V 1L3, Tel (604) 922-1023
Victoria - Boutique de Laine, 2530 Estevan Ave, V8R 2S7 Tel (250) 592-9616
Victoria - Greatest Knits, 1294 Gladstone Ave, V8T 1G6 Tel (250) 386-5523

MANITOBA
Winnipeg - ROWAN AT Ram Wools, 143 Smith Street, R3C 1J5 Tel (204) 942-2797 - MAIL ORDER SERVICE AVAILABLE

NOVA SCOTIA
Dartmouth - Fleece Artist, 1174 Mineville Road, B2Z 1K8 Tel (902) 462-0602

ONTARIO
Ancaster - ROWAN AT The Needle Emporium, 420 Wilson St. East, L9G 4S4. Tel 1 800 667 9167 MAIL ORDER SERVICE AVAILABLE
Belleville - Classic Wool Shop, 169 Albert St, K8N 3N5 Tel (613) 966 6595
Carleton Place - Real Wool Shop, 142 Franktown Road, Box 130. K7C 3P3 Tel (613) 257 2714
Dundas - Rena's Yarns, 6 Sydenham Street. L9H 2T4 Tel (905) 627 2918
Haliburton - Marty's Custom Knits, Box 857, Highland Street, KOM 1SO. Tel (705) 457 3216
Kingston - ROWAN AT The Wool Room, 2-313 University Avenue, K7L 3R3. Tel (613) 544- 9544 or Tel TOLL FREE 1 800 449 5868
Oakville - The Wool Bin, 236 Lakeshore Road East, L6J 1H8 Tel (905) 845 9512

Orillia - Imaginit 2000, 3493 Bayou Road, R R No 3, L3V 6H3 Tel (705) 689-8676
Oshawa - ROWAN AT Alexandra's, 35 Division Street, L1G 5L8 Tel (905) 723-7148
Ottawa. - Woolaine, 1200 St Laurent, G539, K1K 3B8 Tel (613) 745-3094
Ottawa - Your Creation (Jill Andrew), 3767 Mapleshore Drive, (Kemptville) K0G 1J0 Tel (613) 826 3261
Ottawa - Claire's Knitting Place, 1243 Wellington Street, K1Y 3A3 Tel (613) 724-6622
Pembroke - Jane's Wool Studio, 128 Pembroke St. W. K8A 5M8 Tel (613)735-2288
Perth - The Knitting Studio, 2-63 Gore St. E. K7H 1H8 Tel (613) 267-4839
Richmond Hill - ROWAN AT The Hill Knittery, 10720 Yonge St, L4C 3C9 Tel (905) 770-4341 MAIL ORDER SERVICE AVAILABLE , Email: thehillknittery@cheerful.com
Toronto - ROWAN AT Celtic Fox, 1721 Bayview Ave, M4G 3C1 Tel (416) 487-8177 / TOLL FREE (888) 329-3334 Fax (416) 487-9534
Toronto - ROWAN AT Passionknit Ltd, 3467 Yonge Street, M49 2N3 Tel (416) 322-0688 or Fax (416) 864-0984
Toronto - ROWAN AT Romni Wools Ltd, 658 Queen St. West M6J 1E6 Tel (416) 368-0202 MAIL ORDER SERVICE AVAILABLE
Toronto - (The) Wool Mill, 2170 Danforth Avenue, M4C 1K3 Tel (416) 696-2670
Toronto - Village Yarns, 4895 Dundas Street West, M9A 1B2 Tel (416) 232-2361 /www.sympatico.ca/villageyarns
Toronto - (The) Yarn Boutique, 1719A Bloor Street West, M6P 1B2 Tel (416) 760-9129
Toronto - Studio Limestone, 16 Fenwick Ave, M4K 3H3 Tel (416) 469-4018 (MAIL ORDER ONLY)

QUEBEC
Montreal - A la Tricoteuse, 779 Rachel Est, H2J 2H4 Tel (514) 527-2451
Quebec City - Indigo Inc., 155 Rue St. Paul, G1K 3W2 Tel (418) 694-1419
St Lambert - Saute Mouton, 20 Webster, J4P 1N8. Tel (514)671-1155
St Elie d'Orford - Entrepot St Elie, 128 Chemin Dion, J0B 2SO Tel (819) 569-7065
Westmount - Brickpoint Studios, 317-319 Victoria Avenue, H3Z 2L6 Tel (514) 489 0993

SASKATCHEWAN
Saskatoon - Prairie Lily Weavers, #7 1730 Quebec Avenue, S7K 1V9 Tel (306) 665 2771 Fax (306) 343-9095 MAIL ORDER SERVICE AVAILABLE

DENMARK
DISTRIBUTOR: Ruzicka , Hydesbyvej 27, DK4990 Sakskobing. Tel : (45) 54 707804 / www.ruzicka.dk / email: nis@ruzicka.dk

Aabenraa - Garn Cafe, Storegade 6, 6200, Tel 74 62 07 22
Aalborg - ROWAN AT Design Vaerkstedet, Boulevarden 9, 9000 Tel 98 12 07 13
Aalborg - ROWAN AT Fruens Ting, Gravensgade 13, 9000 Tel 98 13 11 12
Aarhus C - ROWAN AT Marianne Isager, Volden 19, 8000, Tel 86 19 40 44
Fano - Kunstladen, Postvej 29, Rindby, 6270 Tel 75 16 35 04
Frederikssund - ROWAN AT Mode Ide Strik & Garn, Falkenborggaarden 2, 3600 Tel 42 31 23 85
Horsens - ROWAN AT Stokvaerket, Smedetorvet 3, 8700 Tel 66 16 01 31
Kobenhavn K - ROWAN AT Sommerfuglen, Vandkunsten 3, 1057 Tel 33 32 82 90
Kobenhavn K - ROWAN AT Uldstedet, Fiolstraede 13, 1171 Tel 33 91 17 71
Koege - Garnladen, Torvet 23, 4600 Tel 53 66 30 50
Lyngby - ROWAN AT Uldstedet, Gl Jernbanevej 7, 2800 Tel 42 88 10 88
Naestved - Butik Unik, Kindhestegade 11, 4700, Tel 53 73 52 07
Nykobing F - Betty Garn, Skolegade 8, 4800 Tel 54 85 05 35
Nykobing M - Nikoline, Blaamunkevej 12, 7900 Tel 97 72 44 74
Odense C - Tante Groen, Vestergade 7, 5000 Tel 66 13 24 48
Odense C - ROWAN AT Flensted, Ramsherred 4, 5000 Tel 66 12 70 44
Randers - Gitte Garn, Sct, Mortensgarde 1, 8900 Tel 86 41 93 11
Ringkobing - Garn, Stof, & Hobby Shoppen, Herningvej 16, 6950 Tel 97 32 60 48
Roskilde - ROWAN AT Garnhoekeren, Karen Olsdatterstraede 9, 4000 Tel 42 37 20 63
Vejle - Arne S. Hansen, Vestergade 45, 7100 Tel 75 82 02 49

FAROE ISLANDS
Torshavn - Hespan, Smyrilsvegur 16, 100 Tel 18 737

GREENLAND
Nuuk - Unik APS, Box 166, Aqqusinersuaq 6, 3900 Tel 2 40 96

FRANCE
DISTRIBUTOR: Elle Tricote, 52 Rue Principale, 67300 Schiltigheim Tel 03 88 62 6531

Annecy - ROWAN AT Od'a'laine, 3 rue Joseph Blanc, 74000. Tel 04 50 51 38 46
Besancon - La Pastourelle, 4 rue Delavelle, 25000. Tel 03 81 80 96 51
Cadenet - Mylene Creations, 14 rue Victor Hugo, 84160 Tel 04 90 77 16 09
Paris (7) - ROWAN AT Le Bon Marche, 115 rue du Bac, 75007. Tel 01 44 39 80 00 Fax 01 44 39 80 50
Paris (8) - Modes & Travaux, 10 rue de la pépinière, 75008 Tel 01 43 87 10 07
Paris(18) - Mme Ceresa, 4 rue Saint Isaure, 75018. Tel 01 42 51 62 37
Ramonville - ROWAN AT Le Sabot des Laines, 15 avenue 'Occitanie, 31520. Tel 05 61 73 14 38
Saint Dié - Tricot Conseil, 11 rue d'Amerique, 88100. Tel 03 29 56 76 16
Saint-Pierre Reunion - Fath Creation, 10 rue Marius et Ary Leblond, 97410. Tel 02 62 96 18 78
Sarzeau - ROWAN AT Les Chemins Buissonniers, 1 Place Marie le Franc, 56370 Tel 02 97 48 08 30
Strasbourg - ROWAN AT Elle tricote, 4 rue de Paques 67000. Tel 03 88 23 03 13 Fax 03 88 23 01 69
Thonon les Bains - ROWAN AT Au Vieux Rouet, 7 rue Ferdinand Dubouloz, 74200. Tel 04 50 71 07 33
Toulon - D'un Fil a L'Autre, 53 rue Jean Jaurès, 83000. Tel 04 94 92 63 76
Tours - Floral Street, 77 rue de la Scellerie, 37000 Tel 02 47 61 38 97 Fax 02 47 61 38 97

GERMANY
DISTRIBUTOR: Wolle & Design, Wolfshovener Strasse 76, 52428 Julich-Stetternich. Tel 02461/54735

Aachen - ROWAN AT Martin Gorg Wolle, Annastrasse 16, 52005 Tel 0241/4705913
Adelsdorf/Aisch - ROWAN AT 'LanArt' Susanne Wettendorf, Hohenstrasse 3, 91325 Tel 09195/50515
Ahrweiler - Dat Laedche, Niederhut Str. 17, 53747 Tel 02641/4464
Augsburg - ROWAN AT Die Mascher - Gertrud Egger , Ludwigstr 4, 86152. Tel : 0821/3495607
Bielefeld-Babenhausen - ROWAN AT Woll-Deele - Reinhild Uffmann, Babenhauser Str. 70, 33619. Tel 0521 887909
Detmold - Die Spindel, Unter der Wehme 5, 32756 Tel 05231/33882
Diedorf - Die Masche - Gerttrud Egger, Kapellenweg 4, 86420. Tel 08238/1433
Hamburg - Woll-Eule - Ilse Jalloul, Frahmredder 7, 22393 Tel 040/6012920
Hamburg - Pur-Pur-Wolle, Hellkamp 9, 20255. Tel 040/4904579
Hannover - ROWAN AT Textilwerkstatt - Minke Heijstra, Friedenstr. 1, 30175. Tel 0511 818001
Itzehoe - Allerhand von Hand - E Seligmann, Oelmuhlengang 2, 25524 Tel 04821/2807
Juelich - ROWAN AT Wolle & Design - R Kaufmann, Wolfshovener Str. 76, 52428 Tel 02461/54735
Kiel - ROWAN AT Wollkaufhaus Markmann, Schonberger Str. 32-34, 24148. Tel 0431/723096
Langen - ROWAN AT Wollwerkstatt - Petra Schoeder, Wassergasse 24, 63225 Tel 06103/22772
Pforzheim Buchenbronn - Wollwerkstatt - M Weinmann, Pforzheimer Str. 8, 75180 Tel 07231/71416
Schallstadt - Senfkorn - A & C Bienger, Erlenweg 16, 79227. Tel 07664/978787
Stuttgart - ROWAN AT Strick Art - Silvia Grosse, Alexanderstr 51, 70182 Tel 0711/245218
Velbert - mit Nadel & Faden - Barbel Hoppe-Abe, Bahnhofstr 21, 42551. Tel : 02051/50712
Wenden - Handarbeiten - B Klur, Severinusstr. 2, 57482 Tel 02762/1351

HOLLAND
DISTRIBUTOR: de Afstap, Oude Leliestraat 12, 1015 AW Amsterdam Tel 020-6231445

Amersfoort - Bombazijn, Kamp 77, 3811 AP. Tel 033-4729949
Amsterdam - de Afstap (Lonnie Bussink), Oude Leliestraat 12, 1015 AW. Tel 020-6231445
Bergen - Finlandia (Vo Haring), Kleine Dorpsstraat 26, 1861 KN. Tel 072-5894642
Bilthoven - Handwerken zonder Grenzen (Henr. Beukers), Nachtegaallaan 18a, 3722 AB. Tel 030-2280930
Haarlem - Wollana (Frieda Smit), Tempeliersstraat 64-68, 2012 EH. Tel 023-5312470
Kilder - Kleur in Kilder, Past. Bluemersstr. 4, 7035 AP. Tel 0314-684657.
Leeuwarden - Atelier Huisvlijt, Noorderweg 18, 8911 ES. Tel 058-2153637
Maarssen - De Draad. Kaatsbaan 30, 3601 ED. Tel 0346-567566
Neerritter - Annemarie Verlinden, Bosstraat 31, 6015 AK. Tel 0475-565984
Roermond - Atelier Fru Holda, Roerderweg 50, 6041 NS. Tel 0475-315929
Someren - Het Weverke, Molenstraat 24, 5711 EW. Tel. 0493-492092
Utrecht - Modilaine (Gerda Aikema), Lijnmarkt 22, 3511 KH. Tel 030-2328911

Rowan Stockists - Overseas

ROWAN DISTRIBUTORS For more information on Overseas Stockists and Mail Order details please contact the Rowan distributor listed under each country

'ROWAN AT ....' stockists who carry a large range of Rowan Yarns

Wormerveer - Priegelmee (J. Hartog), Zaanweg 8, 1521 DH.
Tel 075-6216266
Zierikzee - De Hobbit (Els Mieremet), Paternosterstr./Poststr.
4301 EG. Tel 0111-416786
Zuidlaren - Ryahuis (Lucy van Zanten), Telefoonstraat 26,
9471 EN. Tel 050-4092418

HONG KONG
DISTRIBUTOR: East Unity Company Limited,Room 902,
Block A, Kailey Industrial Centre, 12 Fung Yip Street,
Chai Wan Tel (852) 2869 7110

Macy Wools Co Ltd, Shop 405, City Plaza Stage 1,
Tai Koo Shing, Quarry Bay, Tel 25672678
Kit Kit Wools, Shop 23, 1st Floor, Healey Commercial Complex,
Yuen Long NT Tel 24754292

ICELAND
DISTRIBUTOR: ROWAN AT Storkurinn, Kjorgardi,
Laugavegi 59, ICE -101. Tel 551 82 58

Akranes - Handradinn, Kirkjubraut 3, 300 Akranes
Tel 431 5500
Handid - Ski Pagata, 600 Akureyri Tel 462 4088

ITALY
Rivoli - Victoriana, Via Fratelli Piol 14, (TO) Tel 011 95 32 142

JAPAN
DISTRIBUTOR: Diakeito Co Ltd, 2-3-11 Senba-Higashi,
Minoh City, Osaka 562 Tel 0727 27 6604

LITHUANIA
DISTRIBUTOR: Vakrina's Firm, Vivulskio 7-202,
LT-2600 Vilnius Tel 652801

LUXEMBOURG
Esch/Alzette - Woll-Stuff, Monique Kohnen,
Place Hotel de Ville 12, 4138. Tel 548937

NEW ZEALAND
DISTRIBUTOR: MacEwen Enterprises Ltd,
24b Allright Place, Mt Wellington, Auckland. Tel 09 527 3241

NORWAY
DISTRIBUTOR: Eureka, P.O. Box 357, N-1401 Ski
Tel 64 86 55 40
Dalen - Anne Marit Garnstove, Box 91, 3880 Tel 35 07 70 15
Elverum - Husfliden, St Olausgt 2, 2400 Tel 62 41 13 90
Fevig - Strikkeriet, Fevigtoppen, 4870 Tel 37048410
Kristiansand S - Jonnas Garn & Gaver, Skippergt. 18, 4611.
Tel 38 07 03 95
Oslo - ROWAN AT Husfliden, Mollergt. 4, 0129 Tel 22 42 10 75
Oslo - Colours, Russelokkveien 59, 0251 Tel 22 83 83 66
Sauland - Rett & Vrang, 3692. Tel 35 02 33 66
Ski - ROWAN AT Eureka, Postbox 357, 1400 Tel 64 86 55 40
Stavanger - Olga Evensens Eftf, Laugmannsgt 4, 4006
Tel 51 89 42 66
Aasgaardstrand - **ROWAN AT Eie's Paletten,**
Grev Wedelsgt 46, 3155 Tel 33 04 88 80

SWEDEN
DISTRIBUTOR: Wincent, Norrtullsgatan 65, 113 45
Stockholm Tel (08) 673 70 60
Ahus - P-Perssond and Co, Gamia Skeppsbron 10, 29631
Tel (044) 240121
Goteborg - Nypan, Ekiandagatan 16, 41255 Tel (031) 201037
Gustavsberg - Garnpaletten Gustavsbergshaven,
Odelbergsv 9A, 13440 Tel (08) 510 310 38
Helsingborg - Irmas Hus, Nedra Langvinkelsgatan 15, 25220
Tel (042) 142767
Karlskrona - Cikoria, Amiralitetstorget 27, 37130
Tel (0455) 842 60
Malmo - Irmas Hus, Kalendegatan 13, 21135 Tel (040) 6110800
Orebo - Min Garnbod, Fredsgatan 11, 70362
Tel (019) 6115557
Stockholm -ROWAN AT Wincent, Sveavagen 94, 11350
Tel (08) 673 70 60
Uppsala - Yll & Tyll, Bredgrand 7c, 75320 Tel (018) 105190
Varnamo - Donegal, Storgatsbacken 6, 33000 Tel (0370) 12590

SWITZERLAND
Zurich - Vilfil, Klosbachstrasse 10, Beim Kreuzplatz, 8032
Tel 01 383 99 03

UNITED STATES OF AMERICA
DISTRIBUTOR: Westminster Fibers Inc, 5 Northern
Boulevard, Amherst, New Hampshire 03031
Tel (603) 886 5041/5043. Email: wfibers@aol.com

ALABAMA
Birmingham - The London Knitting Company,
2531 Rocky Ridge Rd, #101, 35243 Tel (205) 822-5855

ALASKA
Anchorage - Knitting Frenzy, 4240 Old Seward Hwy., #18
99503 Tel (907) 563-2717

ARIZONA
Tuscon - Purls, 7862 North Oracle Road, 85704.
Tel (520) 797-8118

CALIFORNIA
Anaheim Hills - ROWAN AT Velona Needlecraft,
5753-B Santa Ana Canyon Road, 92807 Tel (714) 974-1570 /
www.velona.com

Berkeley - ROWAN AT Straw Into Gold, 3006 San Pablo
Avenue, 94702 Tel (510) 548-5243 / www.straw.6216.com/sig
Carmel - ROWAN AT Knitting by the Sea, 5th Ave & Junipero,
93921 Tel (408) 624-3189
Danville - ROWAN AT Filati Yarns, 125 Railroad Ave, Suite D,
94526 Tel (510) 820-6614
Glendale - Village Needleworks, 1413 1/2 W Kenneth Rd, 91201
Tel (818) 507-5990
Los Altos - ROWAN AT Uncommon Threads, 293 State Street,
94022 Tel (415) 941-1815
Oakland - The Knitting Basket, 2054 Mountain Blvd, 94611
Tel (800) 654-4887
Placerville - Placerville Yarn & Needleworks, 327 Main St,
95667 Tel (916) 622-4444
Sacramento - Rumplestiltskin, 1021 R Street, 95814
Tel (916) 442-9225
San Francisco - ROWAN AT Yarn Garden, 545 Sutter St,
Ste 202, 94102. Tel (415) 956-8830 /
www.citysearchch.com/sfo/yarngarden
San Francisco - ROWAN AT Greenwich Yarns,
2073 Greenwich Street, 94123 Tel (415) 567-2535 /
www.citysearch.com/sfo/greenwichyarn
Santa Barbara - Santa Barbara Knitting Studio,
2253, A Las Positas Rd., 93105 Tel (805) 563-4987
Santa Maria - Betty's Fabrics, 1627 So. Broadway, 93454
Tel (805) 922-2181
Santa Monica - L'Atelier on Montana, 1202 Montana Ave 90403
Tel (310) 394-4665 / www.websites.earthlink.net/~latelier
Solana Beach - Common Threads, 531 Stevens Avenue, 92075
Tel (619)481-2112

COLORADO
Boulder - Shuttles, Spindles & Skeins, Inc.,
633 S. Broadway #D, 80303 Tel (303) 494-1071
Denver - ROWAN AT Skyloom Fibers, 1705 S. Pearl, 80210
Tel (303) 777-2331
Estes Park - Bountiful, PO Box 1727, 125B Moraine Ave, 80517
Tel (970) 586-9332

CONNECTICUT
Cheshire - Have You Any Wool, 1101 S Main St, 06410
Tel (203) 699-9644
Westport - ROWAN AT Hook 'N' Needle, 1869 Post Rd East,
06880 Tel (203) 259-5119 / www.hook-n-needle.com
Washington Depot - Featheridge Designs, 4 Green Hill Road,
06794 Tel (800) 371-1014

HAWAII
Honolulu - Yarn Garden 2885 S. King St., Ste 102 96836
Tel (808) 946-0125

ILLINOIS
Chicago - Barkim Ltd. (Mail Order Only) 47 W. Polk St., 60605
Tel (888) 548 - 2211 / www.barkim.com
Chicago - Weaving Workshop, 2218 N Lincoln Ave, 60614
Tel (773) 929-5776
Clarendon Hills - Flying Colours Inc, 154 Burlington, 60514
Tel (630) 325-0888
Elmhurst - Great Yarn Loft, 120 N York Rd, Ste 220, 60126
Tel (630) 833-7423
Evanston - Closeknit Inc, 622 Grove St. 60201
Tel (847) 328 6760
Springfield - Nancy's Knitworks, 1650 W Wabash, Ste I, 62704
Tel (217) 546-0600
St Charles - The Fine Line Creative Arts Center,
6 N. 158 Crane Rd,60175 Tel (630) 584-9443

INDIANA
Ft. Wayne - Cass Street Depot, 1044 Cass Street, 46802
Tel (219) 420-2277
Indianapolis - Mass. Avenue Knit Shop, 521 East North St,
46204 Tel (800) 675-8565

KANSAS
Lawrence - ROWAN AT The Yarn Barn, 930 Mass Ave, 66044
Tel (785) 842-4333

MAINE
Camden -ROWAN AT Stitchery Square, 11 Elm Street, 04843
Tel (207) 236-9773 / www.stitching.com/stitcherysquare
Freeport - ROWAN AT Grace Robinson & Co,
231 US Rte 1 South, 04032 Tel (207) 865-6110

MARYLAND
Baltimore - ROWAN AT Woolworks, 6305 Falls Rd, 21209
Tel (410) 337-9030
Bethseda - ROWAN AT Needlework Attic, 4706 Bethseda Ave,
20814 Tel (800) 654-6654
Bethseda - ROWAN AT Yarns International, 5110 Ridgefield
Road, 20816 Tel (301) 913-2980

MASSACHUSETTS
Boston - Yarnwinder, 247 Newbury St, 02116 Tel (781) 262-0028
Harvard - Bare Hill Studio/Fiber Loft, Rt. 111, P.O. Building.
01451 Tel (800) 874-9276
Lexington - ROWAN AT Wild & Woolly Studio, 7A Meriam St,
02173 Tel (781) 861-7717
Lenox - ROWAN AT Colorful Stitches, 48 Main St. 01240
Tel (800) 413-6111

MICHIGAN
Birmingham - Knitting Room, 251 Merrill, 48009
Tel (248) 540-3623
Plymouth - Old Village Yarn Shop, 42307 Ann Arbor Rd, 48170
Tel (313) 451-0580
Howell - Stitch in Time, 722 East Grand River, 48843
Tel (517) 546-0769
Menominee - Elegant Ewe, 400 First Street, 49858-3308
Tel (906) 863-2296
Traverse City - Lost Art Yarn Shoppe, 123 East Front St.,
49684 Tel (616) 941-1263
Wyoming - Threadbender Yarn Shop - 2767 44th St, SW, 49509
Tel (888) 531-6642

MINNESOTA
Minneapolis - ROWAN AT Linden Hills Yarn, 2720 W. 43rd St,
55410 Tel (612) 929-1255
Minnetonka - Skeins 11309 Highway 7, 55305
Tel (612) 939-4166
St Paul - The Yarnery KMK Crafts, 840 Grand Ave. 55105
Tel 612 222 5793
White Bear Lake - ROWAN AT A Sheepy Yarn Shoppe,
2185 Third St, 55110 Tel (800)480-5462

MONTANA
Stevensville - Wild West Wool, 3920 Suite B Highway 93N,
59870

NEBRASKA
Omaha - ROWAN AT Personal Threads Boutique,
8025 W Dodge Rd, 68114 Tel (402) 391-7733

NEW HAMPSHIRE
Center Harbor - Keepsake Quilting & Country Pleasures,
Senter's Market, Rt. 25, 03226   Tel (800) 865-9458 /
www.keepsakequilting.com
Center Ossipee - ROWAN AT Yarn Express (Mail order only),
120 Moultonville Rd, 03814 Tel (800) 432-1886
Exeter - Charlotte's Web, Exeter Village Shops, 137 Epping Rd,
Rt. 27, 03833 Tel (603) 778-1417

NEW JERSEY
Chatham - Stitching Bee, 240A Main Street, 07928
Tel (201) 635-6691
Garwood - Knitter's Workshop Inc., 345 North Avenue, 07027
Tel (908) 789-1333
Lafayette - Creations, Rte 15, Box 59, Bldg #1,
Olde Lafayette Vlg, 07848 Tel (201) 300-5911
Lambertville - Tomato Factory Yarn Co., 8 Church St, 08530
Tel (800) 483-7959

NEW MEXICO
Albuquerque - Village Wools, 3801 San Mateo Ave, N.E., 87110
Tel (505) 883-2919
Santa Fe - Needles Eye, 927 Paseo de Peralta , 87501
Tel: (505) 982-0706

NEW YORK
Bedford Hills - Lee's Yarn Center, 733 N Bedford Rd, 10507
Tel (914) 244-3400
Brooklyn - ROWAN AT Heartmade (Mail Order only),
521 Third St, 11215 Tel (800) 898-4290
Buffalo - Elmwood Yarn Shop, 1639 Hertel Ave, 14216
Tel (716) 834-7580
Commack - HappiKnits, 6333 Jericho Tpke, 11725
Tel (516) 462-5558
East Hampton - Knitlove, 42 Gingerbread Lane, 11937
Tel (516) 329-0700
Garden City - ROWAN AT Garden City Stitches,
725 Franklin Avenue, 11530
Tel (516) 739-5648
Great Neck - Open Door to Stitchery, 87A Middle Neck Road,
11021 Tel (516) 487-9442
Ithaca - The Homespun Boutique, On The Commons, 14850
Tel (607) 277-0954
Locust Valley - The Wool Shop, 25 The Plaza, 11560
Tel (516) 671-9722
New York City - The Yarn Company, 2274 Broadway, 10024
Tel (212) 787-7878
New York City - ROWAN AT Yarn Connection,
218 Madison Ave, 10016, Tel(212)684-5099
Schenectady - Ye Olde Yarn & Gift Shoppe, 839 McClellan St.,
12304 Tel (518) 393-2695
Skaneateles - ROWAN AT Elegant Needles, 5 Jordan St.,
13152 Tel (315) 685-9276

OHIO
Aurora - Edie's Knit Shop, 215 W. Garfield Rd, 44202
Tel (216) 562-7226
Cincinnati - ROWAN AT Wizard Weavers,
2701 Observatory Rd, 45208
Tel (513) 871-5750
Cleveland - Fine Points, 2026 Murray Hill, 44106
Tel (216) 229-6644
Columbus - Wolfe Fiber Art, 1188 W 5th Ave, 43212
Tel (614) 487-9980
Marion - Abbey Yarns & Kits, 1512 Meyers Road, 43302
Tel (800) 999-5648 / www.abbey-yarns.com

This magazine was photographed on location at The Manor, Hemingford Grey, Huntingdon.

Built about 1130 The Manor is reputedly the oldest continuously inhabited house in the country and was made famous by the author Lucy Boston as the house of Green Knowe in her series of children's books. The house if full of atmosphere from nearly nine centuries of family life.

The garden was laid out by Lucy Boston and contains one of the best collections of old roses in private hands as well as topiary coronation and chess pieces. She also made exquisite patchwork which are on view in the house.

THE MANOR, HEMINGFORD GREY, HUNTINGDON, CAMBS PE18 9BN
The Manor is open to visitors throughout the year by appointment.
Tel: 01480 463134
The garden is open daily between
10am and 6pm

Photography Joey Toller / Styling Kim Hargreaves
Hair & Make-up Claire Ann Ray / Models Helen, Mimi and Michael

---